Born to Lead

Americana Music Trailblazers

Mark Hodermarsky

NEW HAVEN PUBLISHING

Published 2018
New Haven Publishing Ltd
www.newhavenpublishingltd.com
newhavenpublishing@gmail.com

All Rights Reserved
The rights of Mark Hodermarsky, as the author of this work, have been asserted in accordance with the Copyrights, Designs and Patents Act 1988.
No part of this book may be re-printed or reproduced or utilized in any form or by any electronic, mechanical or other means, now unknown or hereafter invented, including photocopying, and recording, or in any information storage or retrieval system, without the written permission of the Author and Publisher.

Cover Photos © John Soeder

Cover design © Pete Cunliffe
pcunliffe@blueyonder.co.uk

Copyright © 2018 Mark Hodermarsky
All rights reserved
ISBN: 978-1-949515-02-2

For my grandchildren

Lily, Henry, and Estelle.

Acknowledgments

My wife, Lynda, who once again provided the support, encouragement, and patience behind another book project.

Chris Hillman, a gifted and treasured artist, whose matchless musical accomplishments, personal integrity, and spirt of adventure continue to inspire listeners after six decades.

Teddy Dahlin, for her steady, hands-on guidance and advice.

Ianthe McGuinn, author of *In the Wings: My Life with Roger McGuinn and the Byrds*, for her lovely Foreword.

John Soeder, for the cover photos.

Sarah Healey, for her superb editing of the text.

Pete Cunliffe, for his brilliance as a graphic designer.

KOOP Radio 91.7 FM (Austin, TX), for permission to reprint portions of their "Genres & Definitions" site.

Steve Traina, radio personality at WCSB-FM in Cleveland, for sharing his encyclopedic knowledge and deep affection for rock and roll with me and so many others.

Brother Mike Hodermarsky, brother-in-law Joe Baker and friends Les Foote, Dan Hess, and Dan Rourke, whose love of music nurtures mine.

Contents

Acknowledgments	5
Foreword by Ianthe McGuinn	8
Introduction	10
What is Americana Music?	13
Bob Dylan	19
The Byrds	29
Gram Parsons	50
Gene Clark	56
Buffalo Springfield	67
The Grateful Dead	74
The Band	82
Arlo Guthrie	97
John Prine	105
Following Their Footsteps	115
Epilogue	154
Glossary of Genres	156
Essential Recordings	164
Bibliography	169
The Author	179

Foreword

References to the 1960s are typically associated with sex, drugs, and rock and roll. Tagging along are peace, love and flower power—all over-played clichés. The truth, in my eyes, is the forgotten innocence of the time. In the United States, we emerged from post-World War II optimism to the realism of the atomic bomb and nuclear fears. It culminated in lost hope with President Kennedy's assassinassion.

Music became the balm that healed us, the youth of the Sixties. The mighty 45-rpm record and the transistor radio were what united us. Folk, R&B, Rockabilly, Rock 'n' Roll—they powered our airwaves and hearts. Buddy Holly, Chuck Berry and the Everly Brothers were adopted by the Brits, and the Beatles took over our American senses.

It was a trans-Atlantic game of musical volleyball. We send the Beach Boys, they return the Beatles, our Dylan their Rolling Stones, our Byrds and they give us the Kinks, and so on...the music always fresh and innovative. We waited for a new Beatles or Dylan album, opening the squeaky cellophane wrap, examining the cover, popping the LP on the turntable, religiously listening to the lyrics and music for encoded secret messages.

In 1968, the Byrds recorded *Sweetheart of the Rodeo*, transfused with Gram Parsons' fresh, passionate approach. They changed the entire genre by electrifying country music the way they had electrified folk music. The fans were confused and preferred Chicago's big band sound. The record had limited success.

When I first met Gram Parsons—stylishly dressed in a leather jacket, hair combed back, lean and tall, ever so graceful—he exuded the seductive charm of a Southern gentleman. His voice, soft and respectful, flowed like a summer mist. His comforting tones enveloped you...a quilt of protective warmth.

Everyone loved Gram; whatever emotional defenses you had melted. His music was mystical, taking you to a far off place, so sorrowful yet lovely and refreshing. Gram's plaintive voice yearned for some discovery or reconciliation, reaching the hollow void in him that needed to be filled.

Emmylou Harris appeared at the right time, complementing his voice and spirit. She probably saved him from an even earlier demise. Their harmonies were pure, tender, deeply loving. Emmy brought out the best in Gram and he provided her a new vocal strength.

Gram died but he gave Emmy the will to survive. Though she struggled without him, the legacy he left was hers. She carried his every sad, haunting note and made it her own. Her music transcended time and has given us the joy in sorrow, the embrace of unfailing love.

I loved the music Emmy created after Gram passed. I knew her manager, Eddie Tickner. He had also managed the Byrds in the early years, when I was married to Roger McGuinn. Emmylou trusted Eddie, and he loved her dearly. She proved to be a lasting friend.

Emmy's music combines the essence of Gram, *Sweetheart of the Rodeo* and Roger's pioneering Folk Rock endeavors. Americana may well be the description of their total contribution. Mark's book brings together the artists and events and chronicles this era of great musical achievement with *Born to Lead: Americana Music Trailblazers*.

Ianthe McGuinn, author of *In the Wings: My Life with Roger McGuinn and The Byrds*

September 2018, Tucson, Arizona.

Introduction

We are especially grateful to those artists who resist convention, who dare to mix seemingly contradictory elements, and who lead rather than follow. To serve as examples, three names come quickly to mind: William Shakespeare, Vincent Van Gogh, and Johann Sebastian Bach. Among their enormous contributions to literature, art, and music is their single most important gift—their incalculable influence on those who attempt to emulate them. Shakespeare's unparalleled understanding of human nature has inspired countless writers across the world; Van Gogh's brilliantly colored palette has been copied by thousands of artists; and Bach's genius at synthesizing various Baroque styles has encouraged composers to incorporate varied (and even dissimilar) musical forms into their compositions.

They were trailblazers.

At the birth of rock 'n' roll in the 1950s, Chuck Berry, Little Richard, Jerry Lee Lewis, Carl Perkins, Elvis Presley, the Everly Brothers, Fats Domino, Buddy Holly, et al, merged R&B, blues, and/or country to create music that stood apart from the mainstream, that invited curiosity and interest, that emboldened throngs of listeners and musicians, and that established a path for 1960s rockers to follow.

They were trailblazers as well.

Born to Lead: Americana Music Trailblazers attempts to identify those artists and bands who, like those mentioned above, have left indelible marks on a particular genre, in this case, Americana music. What exactly (or apparently) is Americana will be the subject of Chapter One.

(Defining this term will be one of my greatest challenges.) I can tell you this much in advance. Between 1965 and 1974, Bob Dylan, the Byrds, Gram Parsons, Gene Clark, Buffalo Springfield, the Grateful Dead, the Band, Arlo Guthrie, and John Prine embodied those traits which define the musical trailblazer. Respectful of traditional American musical forms, their music is nonetheless easily recognizable because of its inventiveness and its adeptness at melding other genres. They created music that was not market-driven, that appealed to the more discerning listener, that found its way more often on independent, album-oriented FM radio rather than on the AM dial, and that inspired future Americana stalwarts—Steve Earle, Lucinda Williams, Townes Van Zandt, Uncle Tupelo, Wilco, Son Volt, Emmylou Harris, and Rodney Crowell, among innumerable others.

Americana, a slippery term to say the least, is a rock genre that owes its growing legions of fans a less ambiguous definition. In addition, a clearer account of Americana's origins should help us more easily recognize its distinctive features while providing an opportunity to honor nine gifted ancestors, who not only fashioned Americana, but who also altered the course of rock history. These trailblazers mapped routes that display the most endearing characteristics of the best that rock and roll offers, including, and perhaps most importantly, pushing musical boundaries. A chief dynamic in their stories and subsequent legacies is their restlessness, their unwillingness to embrace the status quo, their spirit of musical adventure.

They were born to lead.

What is Americana Music?

"If you can taste the dirt through your ears, that is Americana."
(Jed Hilly)

The music today referred to as "Americana" has been around since Bob Dylan strapped his Fender Stratocaster over his shoulder in 1965 and probably even earlier. We can't know for certain. Discovering the exact origin of any musical genre has proven unsolvable. Who actually invented country? Blues? Rhythm & blues? Rock and roll? Good luck finding the answer. We can, however, identify those artists who popularized an original sound that caught the interest of listeners while inspiring multitudes of musicians to model: Hank Williams (country), Robert Johnson (blues), Louis Jordan (R&B), Chuck Berry (rock 'n' roll).

Just what is Americana? A good place to start is the official definition from the Americana Music Association (AMA):

> Americana is contemporary music that incorporates elements of various American roots music styles, including country, roots-rock, folk, bluegrass, R&B and blues, resulting in a distinctive roots-oriented sound that lives in a world apart from the pure forms of the genres upon which it may draw. While acoustic instruments are often present and vital, Americana also often uses a full electric band.

Founded in 1999, each year the AMA holds a national conference, AMERICANAFEST, and annually produces the Americana Music Honors & Awards, which honors and awards members of the Americana music community. Both events attract thousands to Nashville, TN. "If you can taste the dirt through your ears, that is Americana," says AMA executive director, Jed Hilly, who is responsible for having "Americana" included in the *Merriam-Webster Collegiate Dictionary* ("a genre of American music having roots in early folk and country music") and for persuading the Recording Academy to recognize Americana with Grammy categories, including "Best Americana Album."

Contributing to a *No Depression* magazine article, "How Do You Define Americana Music?" Harry Lipson believes that "Americana music is the fertile ground where Rock, Roots, Bluegrass, Celtic, Southern Rock, Appalachian, 'Austin alternative country,' Folk and the Delta blues collide and flourish." Closely related to Lipson's definition is this one from rateyourmusic.com:

> Americana is an amalgam of roots music fused by the confluence of the shared and varied traditions that make up the American musical ethos; specifically those sounds that are merged from folk, country, rhythm & blues, rock & roll and other external influential styles. Americana is popularly referred to, especially in print, as alt-country or sometimes alt.country.

Others find it easier to define Americana by emphasizing that which it is not. From the same *No Depression* piece, Frank Kocher says, "I don't get an Americana vibe from most jazz music, electronica, hip hop/rap, progressive rock, and hard/metal rock without a blues base. Like someone said, you know it when you hear it: Rory Gallagher, yes;

King Crimson, no. The Band, yes; Spiro Gyra, no." Americana artists are not heard on mainstream, commercial radio because they don't fit neatly into specific genres. Americana performers rarely utilize high-tech instruments or production techniques and often play in small venues without lavishly decorated sets or dazzling pyrotechnics. Intimacy and simplicity are the main ingredients.

Americana artist Jimmie Faden of the Dirt Band, as quoted by Michael Scott Cain, points to another distinguishing quality of the Americana musician, the music rather than the compensation for playing the music is of more importance:

> Americana doesn't pay as much as some fields, but we've always been able to work and make money at a level that has made us somewhat comfortable. There's always been people who wanted to see us play, and that's given us enough to have homes and put our kids through school. Nothing exorbitant but enough. We're able to continue to create and play music for the people who want to hear it.

Many have criticized the word "Americana" because of its vagueness, claiming the term to be too broad an umbrella, that it is much too inclusive. Some complain that its boundaries are not readily understood. The patriotic undertone of the word bothers some, as does our incessant desire to fit things into categories, particularly those items that oppose classification.

Some prefer these terms to Americana: alternative country (alt-country), country rock, roots music, roots fusion, Cosmic American Music (Cosmic Americana), and cosmic country. Americana's sub-genres include gothic Americana, folk rock, psychedelic country, psychedelic

Americana, progressive country, and outlaw country. These musical styles are, at the very least, sub-genres of Americana. Jimmie Fadden, again from his interview with Michael Scott Cain, speculates that "Americana was an attempt [by the AMA] to group together a lot of unexplainable roots music in a way that could be encapsulated, presented to an audience, with an understanding of it having a name." The AMA has successfully built a home for Americana's expanding popularity.

What seems clear is that Americana is roots-based, genre-bending, and more influenced by country/bluegrass than R&B. Americana artists make the music they wish to make without regard for airplay on commercial radio. To arrive at a universal definition of Americana is not possible, but we seem to know it when we hear it performed by the following: Mary Chapin Carpenter, Gillian Welch, the Avett Brothers, Lucinda Williams, Old Crow Medicine Show, Neil Young, the Mavericks, Alison Kraus, the Jayhawks, Dwight Yoakam, John Hiatt, Buddy Miller, Alabama Shakes, T-Bone Burnett, and Emmylou Harris. Note the musical diversity represented here.

Conversely, Rascal Flatts, Keith Urban, Taylor Swift, Carrie Underwood, Kenny Chesney, Lady Antebellum, Tim McGraw, Alabama, Florida Georgia Line, Sugarland, Garth Brooks, Cole Swindell, Blake Shelton, Maren Morris, the Band Perry, and Faith Hill fall plainly under the country pop heading. The genre-blurring quality of Americana is not apparent. Straying beyond the borders of what mainstream country music requires will not get your record on the radio. Country pop is vigorously formulaic in its structure and production whereas Americana permits and encourages the artist to experiment with combining any number of styles into the mix.

Today's mainstream country performers play music that is unrecognizable from the songs of country/bluegrass pioneers: the Carter Family, Jimmie Rodgers, Roy Acuff, Hank Williams, Bill Monroe, Doc Watson, Earl Scruggs, Buck Owens, Marty Robbins, Bob Wills, George Jones, Loretta Lynn, Merle Haggard, Johnny Cash, and others. On the other hand, Americana musicians will not hesitate to sip from country music's sacred spring for inspiration.

Many performers have embraced the straightjacketed control by mainstream country record producers, but just as many have rejected the prescribed homogeneity. Discerning listeners, those who appreciate and derive pleasure from music that does not pander to pretentiousness, posturing, and predictability, frequently choose Americana as their go-to contemporary music genre. Americana record promoter Al Moss asserts that Americana is "based on American roots traditions. That can really encompass a pretty wide range of music. It means authentic music with integrity to me as opposed to a 'manufactured product.'" The musical integrity that permeates Americana hooks listeners.

Indeed, "Americana" is a very subjective term, with few people defining the genre in like words. Ironically, that is its principal strength. Ranker.com ranks the top 50 Americana artists on its site, and last.fm lists well over 500 Americana artists on its site. I might not have included the same names on these respective rosters, but I admire the scale, depth, and accounts of the choices offered to readers. As a result, I am driven to explore these artists, to hear how they've endeavored to combine a variety of musical styles to deliver an original, non-mainstream sound. I want to "taste the dirt through [my] ears." I also will be listening for echoes from the Americana trailblazers who preceded them, without whom these compositions might not have been possible, whose signatures still find their way into songs at least 50 years later.

A final word. Those artists pictured on the book's cover (Tom Petty, Jackson Brown, Sheryl Crow, John

Mellencamp and Crosby, Stills and Nash) have all been recognized by the AMA for their contributions to the Americana movement even though most critics would not label them specifically as Americana artists. The fact is that all have been inspired in some way by the nine trailblazers and have themselves influenced a multitude of rock and rollers.

Bob Dylan

"Bob Dylan was a guy that came along
when I was twelve or thirteen and just
changed all the rules about what it meant to
write songs."
(Jackson Browne)

It is impossible to overstate Bob Dylan's contributions to both contemporary music and popular culture. Let us not forget that he won the Nobel Prize in Literature in 2016. Proclaimed "The Voice of a Generation" because of his 1960s protest songs, Dylan also is credited by many with inventing folk rock, country rock, and Americana.

Born Robert Allen Zimmerman (he changed his name when he left for college) in Duluth, Minnesota in 1941 and raised in Hibbing, Minnesota, Dylan as a teenager, inspired by Little Richard, Elvis Presley, Hank Williams, Woody Guthrie, and Robert Johnson, put together several high school bands. While performing the hit single "Rock and Roll Is Here to Stay" by Danny & the Juniors at a high school dance, the music "was so loud that the principal cut the microphone," according to author Howard Sounes. A more lasting effect on 17-year-old Dylan was seeing Buddy Holly at the Duluth Armory on January 31, 1959, three days before Holly's tragic death in a plane crash. As Dylan conveyed in his Nobel Lecture, "He [Holly] looked me straight dead in the eye, and he transmitted something. Something I didn't know what. And it gave me the chills."

Spending his childhood and adolescence in a tightly-knit Jewish community, Dylan was well aware of the anti-Semitism faced by his grandparents in Ukraine (Odessa at the time) and Lithuania, and he certainly became familiar with the hostility directed towards Jews in this country. There can be little doubt how Dylan's Jewishness shaped his songwriting. In his early songs especially, Dylan repeatedly assails ignorance, intolerance, injustice, prejudice, and racism.

After dropping out of the University of Minnesota, where he played folk music in local coffeehouses, he headed to New York City where he met a seriously ill Woody Guthrie, his idol, who Dylan described as "the true voice of American spirit"; he promised himself, according to Sounes, that he "was going to be Guthrie's greatest disciple."

Gaining a growing following among the Greenwich Village folk community, Dylan signed a recording contract with Columbia Records, and his self-titled first album, *Bob Dylan*, was released in 1962. Only two original compositions, the most memorable being his tribute to Woody Guthrie, "Song to Woody," appeared on the record, with traditional folk songs dominating the tracks.

After the lukewarm reception from critics and the public for Dylan's first album, the response for his next, *The Freewheelin' Bob Dylan*, which included only two covers, was astounding. With its 1963 release, Bob Dylan's name became known to millions because of the widely played and controversial protest songs— "Blowin' in the Wind," "Masters of War," "A Hard Rain's a-Gonna Fall," and "Oxford Town," and for two classic love songs—"Girl from the North Country" and "Don't Think Twice, It's All Right." The lyrical craftsmanship, ingenious wordplay, fierce social commentary, and unique vocal phrasing instantly catapulted Dylan to major artist status. As Richard Williams writes: "For [college] students whose exam courses included Eliot and Yeats, here was something that flattered their expanding intellect while appealing to the teenage rebel in their early-sixties souls. James Dean had walked around reading James Joyce; here were both in a single package, the words and the attitude set to music."

"This is rich, imaginative music," declares reviewer Stephen Thomas Erlewine, "capturing the sound and spirit of America as much as that of Louis Armstrong, Hank Williams, or Elvis Presley. Dylan, in many ways, recorded music that equaled this, but he never topped it." Perhaps no other contemporary musical artist has ever elevated his or her "game" to this degree in so short a time. *Freewheelin'* proved to be a transcendent moment in music.

Bob Dylan's next album, the 1964 *The Times They Are a-Changin'*, like its predecessor offered more anthems—"The Times They Are a-Changin'," "With God on Our Side," "Only a Pawn in Their Game," and "The Lonesome Death of Hattie Carroll." With these two albums, Dylan not only transformed the role of the singer-songwriter but also changed popular culture, as author Sean Wilentz points out:

> He [Dylan] is the most important songwriter of the last 50 years . . . Then there's the '60s. Dylan's work is indelibly linked to that time, in part because so much of his greatest work came out of '64, '65, '66 . . . Jim Crow was smashed, the beginnings of the movements that would end communism in Eastern Europe—all sorts of things were happening all around the world in the late 1960s, throughout the 1960s. And his music was very much a part of that. It expressed what he wanted to express, but people caught onto it as an expression of what they were feeling, what they were thinking.

From his article, "Bob Dylan's Influence on the Beatles," Aaron Krerowicz believes that Dylan influenced the Beatles in two ways: introducing them to marijuana and freeing "them from the conventions of pop music." Dylan's impact resulted "in an increased use of acoustic rather than electric instruments in Beatles recordings, as well as a dramatic rise in their compositional craftsmanship." As John Lennon states, as quoted by Krerowicz:

> I had a sort of professional songwriter's attitude to writing pop songs. We would turn out a certain style of song for a single . . . I'd have a separate songwriting John Lennon who wrote songs for the meat market, and I didn't consider them (the lyrics or anything)

> to have any depth at all . . . Then I started being me about the songs, not writing them objectively, but subjectively . . . I'd started thinking about my own emotions . . . Instead of projecting myself into a situation, I would try to express what I felt about myself . . . It was Dylan who helped me realise that.

Bob Dylan's anthem-writing days came to a close with his next four albums—*Another Side of Bob Dylan, Bringing It All Back Home, Highway 61 Revisited*, and *Blonde on Blonde*—but his impact on contemporary music only surged. These 1964-1966 recordings, especially the last three, reveal the artistic restlessness of a musical trailblazer in full force.

Bringing It All Back Home (1965) is divided into two sides, electric and acoustic, a decision that alienated him from the folk community but which signaled a new era. *Rolling Stone* magazine reporter Will Hermes claims that with this record Dylan not only invented folk rock but "conjured performances that would completely reimagine how pop music communicated—not just what it could say, but how it could say it . . . [the record] was the cultural equivalent of a nuclear bomb." The electrified "Subterranean Homesick Blues" (the first rap record many say) and "Maggie's Farm" uniquely incorporate blues, R&B, electric blues, and Chuck-Berry rock, while the acoustic "Mr. Tambourine Man" and "Gates of Eden" stand as two of the most lyrically brilliant compositions in rock history.

On the next studio album, released in 1965, *Highway 61 Revisited*, Dylan went totally electric and generated more critical acclaim with arguably his finest song, "Like a Rolling Stone." Indeed, *Rolling Stone* magazine ranked it at #1 in their "500 Greatest Songs of All Time" list. Bruce Springsteen was no less smitten with the recording:

> The first time I heard Bob Dylan, I was in the car with my mother listening to WMCA, and on came that snare shot that sounded like somebody'd kicked open the door to your mind . . . The way that Elvis freed your body, Dylan freed your mind, and showed us that because the music was physical did not mean it was anti-intellect. He had the vision and talent to make a pop song so that it contained the whole world. He invented a new way a pop singer could sound, broke through the limitations of what a recording could achieve, and he changed the face of rock 'n' roll for ever and ever.

At 6 minutes and 13 seconds, "Like a Rolling Stone," despite efforts by record executives to shorten it, also became the longest pop song ever played, changing for all time the conventional "less-than-three-minutes" parameter.

Well worth mentioning is Dylan's much-discussed performance at the 1965 Newport Folk Festival on July 25, where he outraged most in the audience and several fellow folk singers by playing a set of electrified songs during his first set, including "Maggie's Farm" and "Like a Rolling Stone." On a tour that same year, backed by the Hawks (later called the Band), Dylan endured steady abuse from concertgoers as drummer Levon Helm recalls:

> We were booed everywhere; by then it had become a ritual. People had heard they were "supposed" to boo when those electric guitars came out . . . people came out front yelling, "Get rid of the band!" and backstage, people coming up to Bob and saying –right in front of us sometimes—"Look, Bobby,

>these bums [the Hawks] are *killing* you. They're destroying your career. You're getting *murdered* out there. Why do you want to pollute the purity of your thing with this *dirty*, *vulgar*, rock and roll?"

A year later, he would be bombarded with jeers from patrons and hostile reviews from the press during the second, electric set in most cities during a 1966 world tour. In London's Royal Albert Hall a person in the balcony yelled "*Judas*!" and Dylan responded with "You're a fuckin' liar" and then ordered his bandmates to "play fuckin' loud." To his credit, Dylan would not back down. He never succumbed to the pressure. He understood before anyone else that traditional folk music was becoming increasingly anachronistic. The trailblazer in him insisted that he seek untraveled musical paths.

By 1966 Bob Dylan was recognized by most commentators as rock music's most creative and influential force. The release of *Blonde on Blonde* that year punctuated that perception. One of rock music's first double albums, the genre blending apparent since *Bringing It All Back Home* is at the forefront as are the startlingly original lyrics. Of special merit are "Visions of Johanna," "Stuck Inside of Mobile with the Memphis Blues Again," "Just Like a Woman," and the controversial single "Rainy Day Women #12 & 35," which some interpreted as a drug song. Recorded in both New York City and Nashville, Dylan was backed by an array of talented musicians—the Hawks, Al Kooper, Joe South, and Kenny Buttrey. Jazz, blues, and rock magnificently merged with rock and roll's most visionary writing to date.

One of rock's greatest mysteries involves the true details behind Bob Dylan's serious motorcycle accident on July 29, 1966. Rumors of death and permanent brain damage circulated. Dylan luckily survived but with injuries to his vertebrae that would stop the hectic lifestyle brought on by constant recording and touring. He would not go on the road for another eight years. Quietness and domesticity replaced the grueling rock-star, celebrity pace. Nonetheless, following his convalescence Dylan recorded more than a hundred songs with the Band at Big Pink, a house in Saugerities, New York near Dylan's suburban home outside of Woodstock. Those songs would eventually (1975) land on *The Basement Tapes* album and be recognized as the first definitive example of Americana music.

The motorcycle accident and lifestyle changes dramatically impacted Bob Dylan's artistic path. Unlike his last three studio albums, the 1967 *John Wesley Harding* replaced the abstract lyricism, cynical tone, hard-driving electric blues formula with a (mostly) plainspoken, sparsely arranged, country-tinged, roots-infused sound. Only three musicians played with Dylan, in contrast to the flock assisting on recent LPs. While so many popular rock artists were experimenting with psychedelia, including the Beach Boys *(Pet Sounds)* and Beatles (*Sgt. Pepper's Lonely Heart Club Band*), trailblazer Dylan carved a different path and in the process became an Americana forefather. Reviewing the album, Gordon Mills concludes, "Without a doubt this is another major musical step for Bob Dylan. The predominance of country blues, white and black, from Hank Williams to Leadbelly is unprecedented in the new electric music. The steel guitar conjures shades of the Black Ace on many a front porch down South."

Though similarly textured, *John Wesley Harding* invoked greater lyrical complexity ("All Along the Watchtower," "The Ballad of Frankie Lee and Judas Priest," to name two) and more folk elements than did his next album, *Nashville Skyline* (1969), an unabashedly country music record. Here Dylan gently croons rather than sings in simple, direct words as in "Lay Lady Lay," "To Be Alone with You," and "Tonight I'll Be Staying Here with You."

The most consequential cut on the album is Bob Dylan's duet with Johnny Cash on "Girl from the North Country." This song beautifully and forever bridged the gap between the country music and rock and roll establishments, as Kris Kristofferson states:

> Our generation owes him [Dylan] our artistic lives because he opened all the doors in Nashville when he did *Blonde on Blonde* and *Nashville Skyline*. The country scene was so conservative until he arrived. He brought in a whole new audience. He changed the way people thought about it—even the Grand Ole Opry was never the same again.

On the very first episode (June 7, 1969) of what would turn out to be both a popular and musically groundbreaking TV show, *The Johnny Cash Show*, Cash introduced as his first musical guest Bob Dylan, who sang "I Threw It All Away" and later, with Cash, "Girl from the North Country." Joni Mitchell also was featured on Cash's debut show, which was taped at the Ryman Auditorium in Nashville. Cash, idolized by traditional country fans, risked harming his fan base by inviting non-country (or perceived politically left) artists on future episodes as Neil Young, Linda Ronstadt, Odetta, Creedence Clearwater Revival, Pete Seeger, Joe Tex, the Monkees, the Staple Singers, Ray Charles, and Arlo Guthrie. The musical diversity represented by the range of guests and genres on the show strongly suggests that *The Johnny Cash Show* offered the first national stage for the Americana artist.

Dylan has influenced every rock artist from the Beatles to the Avett Brothers for his peerless songwriting, originality, and genre-bending, formula-breaking, risk-taking approach to musical composition. Even at age 77 he still tours the world, often preferring to perform in small, intimate venues rather than large concert halls.

Although many were stunned by his winning the 2016 Nobel Prize for Literature "for having created new poetic expressions within the great American song tradition," a closer examination of his craftsmanship reveals a truly remarkable poet. As Mikal Gilmore from *Rolling Stone* magazine remarked:

> This is what great writers [like Dylan] do, no matter the era. They tell us where we've been, where we are, where we might be headed, as we make our way down timeless and sometimes unfriendly roads. They scar, enlighten and liberate us, they give us unending meanings in new language that help make sense of our world. This is what Bob Dylan does now, as masterfully as he did in 1965 and 1966. This is why he has become America's greatest writer, in any genre. This is why he won the Nobel Prize, and this is why we celebrate this moment.

Artists Who Influenced Bob Dylan

Elvis Presley, Woody Guthrie, Jimmie Rodgers, Doc Watson, Johnny Cash, Hank Williams, Buddy Holly, Robert Johnson, Bill Monroe, Ramblin' Jack Elliot Lead Belly, Blind Willie McTell, and the Weavers.

Americana Artists Influenced by Bob Dylan

John Prine, Joe Ely, John Hiatt, Emmylou Harris, the Jayhawks, Rodney Crowell, Mary Chapin Carpenter, Steve Earle, Sheryl Crow, Townes Van Zandt, Nick Lowe, Tom Petty, Jonah Tolchin, Deleted Scenes, Gillian Welch, and Billy Bragg.

The Byrds

"The original Byrds were very much Beatles-influenced, and then we gradually got our own sound. We started mixing things more."
(Roger McGuinn)

That the Byrds are regarded by critics as America's most influential rock band should not be surprising. The Beatles famously called the Byrds their favorite American group and learned a thing or two from them. From their rock and roll covers of Bob Dylan's "Mr. Tambourine Man," "All I Really Want to Do," "Chimes of Freedom," and "My Back Pages" emerged the genre folk rock. Between 1964 and 1973 the Byrds also blazed musical trails in jangle pop, psychedelic rock, raga rock, and country rock. Pathfinding Americana artists—Gene Clark, the Flying Burrito Brothers, and Gram Parsons—were spawned from the Byrds.

Folk singers Roger McGuinn (recognized earlier as Jim McGuinn), Gene Clark, and David Crosby, met at the Troubadour in Los Angeles in 1964, began harmonizing and, excited by the result, quickly formed a trio, calling themselves the Jet Set. The Beatles had exploded onto the rock scene and totally seduced the threesome, individually and collectively. (Interestingly, at the start of their popularity the Byrds were nicknamed the "American Beatles.") As David Crosby, from Andrew Grant Jackson's book *1965*, remembers:

> McGuinn had been trying to figure out how the Beatles got their sound. Then when the trio went to a screening of *A Hard Day's Night*, he spotted George Harrison's brand-new twelve-string Rickenbacker. "That's it!" he exclaimed. Crosby recalled, "We knew exactly what we wanted to do. It probably blew my mind more than [the Beatles' appearance on] *Ed Sullivan*. The whole movie was magic. I'm told that I came out of the theater, grabbed a stop sign and swung around it like I was pole dancing. I was just so happy. It was like, 'Oh, man . . . I know how to do that!'" Folk singers were supposed

to use only acoustic twelve-strings, but McGuinn went out and bought his own electric Rickenbacker.

Needing a drummer and bassist the Jet Set added Michael Clarke, who was hired more for his Beatles/Brian Jones-style haircut than for his drumming, and Chris Hillman, who played mandolin in a number of bluegrass bands. Although Clarke's drumming skills would remain questionable at best, Hillman would soon develop into an extraordinary bassist and key songwriter.

The 1965 release of their debut album, *Mr. Tambourine Man*, immediately established the Byrds as international rock stars. The single "Mr. Tambourine Man" climbed all the way to number #1 on both the *Billboard* Hot 100 and the United Kingdom (UK) lists. Their blending of folk with rock no doubt influenced mid-1960s contemporaries Simon & Garfunkel, the Turtles, the Mamas & the Papas, and others.

A Pete Seeger cover "Turn! Turn! Turn!" from the band's second LP release of that year, *Turn! Turn! Turn!*, topped the *Billboard* chart and contained more original material than the first album, including three from the member who was becoming the group's most respected songwriter, Gene Clark. Clark had composed one of the Byrds' most enduring songs, "I'll Feel a Whole Lot Better," on the first record. The second album again showcased the multi-layered harmonies, jangling guitar sounds, and perceptive lyrics that distinguished the group from their peers and that has been copied but never surpassed. Of special note are the Byrds' earliest attempts to record a country music song, Porter Wagoner's "Satisfied Mind," and the ambitious covers of Dylan's "Lay Down Your Weary Tune" and "The Times They Are a-Changin'." As reviewer Beverly Patterson comments:

Strewn with socially conscious prose and a thoughtful tone that's equal parts moody and positive, *Turn! Turn! Turn!* captures both the political and musical climate of the hour it was conceived. Ever the sonic scientists, the Byrds went on to pioneer psychedelia, followed by country rock. Not only were they one of the most adventurous bands of the '60s, but their influence is as strong now [2015] as it was then. Crisp, smart and exuding empathy, *Turn! Turn! Turn!* is the ultimate folk-rock memento designed to stimulate the mind, grip the heart and sing along with.

Though rock had surpassed folk as the younger generation's musical preference by the mid-60s, the social commentary that the likes of Woody Guthrie, Pete Seeger, Phil Ochs, and Bob Dylan infused in their acoustic songs became more "amplified." The additions of a drum kit, electric bass, electric guitar, (perhaps) keyboards, and a rock and roll swagger heightened the intensity of the performance and importance of the lyrics. Rock artists could and did rally listeners to the issues of the day in songs that might even translate into hit singles: Barry McGuire's "Eve of Destruction," the Turtles' "Let Me Be," and Simon & Garfunkel's "The Sound of Silence." With "Mr. Tambourine Man" and "Turn! Turn! Turn!" the Byrds demonstrated that a thematically and lyrically rich song could be commercially profitable and that an artist need not sacrifice musical integrity to engage a wider audience.

Fifth Dimension, the Byrds' third album, did not fly up the 1966 charts as had the previous two, but over time its reputation has grown largely because of its contribution to psychedelic rock. As was the situation with Bob Dylan, who ushered in the folk-rock era with *Bringing It All Back Home*, the Byrds chose, like Dylan, to seek new musical adventures by incorporating sounds rarely heard on rock recordings—psychedelic sounds. In the process, the Byrds followed an Americana tenet—allow your heart rather than a record company to be your guide.

The use of recreational drugs by folk, jazz, blues, and rock musicians during the mid-60s is widely documented. The Byrds and the Beatles were among the many bands who experimented with psychedelic drugs, especially LSD, to achieve spiritual enlightenment and to inspire musical creativity. "Eight Miles High" from *Fifth Dimension* was released as a single and immediately garnered controversy by being banned by some radio stations because of lyrics that supposedly endorsed the use of LSD. The band denied these allegations, stating that the words described an airplane flight to London and not an LSD trip. On "Eight Miles High" Roger McGuinn imitates the sound of free-form jazz legend John Coltrane with his 12-string Rickenbacker while the vocals echo the Indian (raga) music of Ravi Shankar. However, in a 2014 interview with Dave Simpson of *The Guardian*, David Crosby said, "Of course 'Eight Miles High' was a drug song. It does refer to the altitude of that flight, but it was a deliberate double entendre."

A *Psychedelic Sight* article provides the following observations regarding the importance of *Fifth Dimension* to the psychedelic rock genre:

> In July of 1966, *Fifth Dimension* stood alone. The Beatles had not yet released *Revolver*. The Jefferson Airplane *Surrealistic Pillow* was seven months off. Pink Floyd, the Grateful Dead, and Country Joe and the Fish had yet to record their first albums. Psychedelic music was mostly a rumor. Until *Fifth Dimension* . . . The cluttered, borderline

dissonant instrumental sections [in "Eight Miles High"] were unprecedented in rock & roll . . . "2-4-2 Fox Trot (The Lear Jet Song)" incorporates the whine of jet engines and in-flight radio chatter. This repetitive bit of business was ahead of its time in use of non-musical sonic elements.

Flexing their musical versatility on *Fifth Dimension*, in addition to psychedelic rock the Byrds offer listeners traditional folk ("Wild Mountain Thyme" and "John Riley"), country rock ("Mr. Spaceman"), garage rock ("Hey Joe"), and R&B ("Captain Soul"). Two additional notes of interest—no Bob Dylan covers and Gene Clark's departure. Whether it was Clark's renowned fear of flying, David Crosby's unrelenting arrogance, or his bandmates' jealousy as to the hefty amounts of money he was earning from his songwriting, the reasons remain unclear. Clark left the band after participating on only two of the album's songs, "Eight Miles High," which he chiefly wrote, and the instrumental "Captain Soul."

With Clark's exodus bassist Chris Hillman upped his game by composing four songs of his own ("Have You Seen Her Face," "Time Between," "Thoughts and Words," and "The Girl with No Name") and co-writing another ("So You Want to Be a Rock 'n' Roll Star") and adding four lead vocals on the 1967 *Younger Than Yesterday* album. Hillman's bluegrass and country and western roots emerge, no doubt shaping the future musical direction (country rock) of the Byrds.

The musical eclecticism of *Fifth Dimension* returns in the much-acclaimed *Younger Than Yesterday*. *Rolling Stone* magazine listed it as one of its "50 Essential Albums of 1967" for these reasons:

Younger Than Yesterday was the Byrds' first mature album, a blend of space-flight twang and electric hoedown infused with the imminent glow of 1967 yet underlined with crackling realism. The galloping "So You Want to Be a Rock 'n' Roll Star" mocked overnight success, including the Byrds' own (the teen screams were taped at their own gigs). Crosby's ballad "Everybody's Been Burned" hinted at the stress that soon culminated in his firing. And in "My Back Pages," McGuinn's stoic vocal captured the crisis and experience in Bob Dylan's lyrics, a lesson reflected in his own determination to keep the band alive.

David Crosby would call *Younger Than Yesterday* his "favorite Byrds album of all."

Dylan's *John Wesley Harding* and *Nashville Skyline* influenced Americana as much as any of his recordings, as did the next two Byrds' albums, *The Notorious Byrd Brothers* and *Sweetheart of the Rodeo*, both released in 1968.

The experimental period for the Byrds reached its zenith with the release of *The Notorious Byrd Brothers*. Here the band emulates recent efforts at blending psychedelic rock, folk rock, jazz, and country. They also add for the first time a pedal steel guitar (played by the legendary Red Rhodes) and Moog synthesizer (played by its inventor Robert Moog and Roger McGuinn). The album represents Crosby's farewell—he was fired just before its release. Drummer Michael Clarke was also fired after the recording sessions ended. Former member and foremost songwriter Gene Clark returns (temporarily) but pens only one song (with Roger McGuinn), "Get to You."

Despite the tension surrounding the production, the Byrds just may have recorded their finest work. The following songs stand out: "Artificial Energy," "Goin' Back," "Draft Morning," "Wasn't Born to Follow," and "Old John Robertson."

In "Artificial Energy" a horn section powerfully captures the effect of a drug taker's amphetamine rush and its terrible consequences. "Goin' Back" offers some of the band's most lustrous harmonies. The anti-war "Draft Morning" effectively incorporates battlefield sound effects to heighten the narrator's (soldier's) predicament. Made famous by its appearance on the soundtrack of the 1969 anti-establishment blockbuster hit, *Easy Rider*, "Wasn't Born to Follow," could be the first and clearest example of psychedelic country with lyrics preaching individual freedom accompanied by the dazzling interplay of Red Rhodes' pedal steel and Clarence White's electric guitar. As session players on the recording, neither Rhodes nor White were band members. White would soon, however, be asked to join the Byrds. The country-tinged "Old John Robertson" employs two studio effects, phasing and flanging, along with orchestral elements, to add a unique and surprisingly complementary psychedelic edge.

Speaking of psychedelic, among the surplus of definitions for Americana music rarely, if ever, does the word "psychedelic" appear. That is unfortunate. Not only did the Byrds make folk music danceable, they also proved that psychedelic music and country music are not incompatible. Indian instrumentation, extended instrumental solos, unusual recording techniques and surreal lyricism found a happy home with the Byrds and other bands who followed their lead: Jefferson Airplane, the Flying Burrito Brothers, Buffalo Springfield, New Riders of the Purple Sage, the Grateful Dead, Tom Petty and the Heartbreakers, Beachwood Sparks, the Jayhawks, R.E.M., Son Volt, Wilco, and Futurebirds. Actually, the "Cosmic

American Music" term (described in detail later) that Gram Parsons coined fits the Byrds and their descendants as well as if not better than "Americana."

The first country rock album? Bob Dylan's *Nashville Skyline*? *Safe at Home* by the International Submarine Band? *The Gilded Palace of Sin* by the Flying Burrito Brothers? The Beau Brummels' *Bradley's Barn*? Dillard & Clark's *The Fantastic Expedition of Dillard & Clark*? Technically, *Safe At Home*, as it was released before the others. But the major contender for the title "most influential" country rock LP, perhaps the undisputed champion, belongs to the Byrds' *Sweetheart of the Rodeo*.

"Groundbreaking" is much too feeble a word to describe *Sweetheart*'s importance to country rock and Americana. But, at the time, the Byrds' decision to turn away from a distinctive, much admired, and successful musical style seemed foolish. Here was a band who risked alienating legions of fans across the world and potentially a sizable income from record sales to make a traditional country album minus the psychedelia, jangling guitars, and imaginative lyrics. The counter-culture would not approve—hippies and "rednecks" did not mix, it was assumed.

Roger McGuinn, as quoted by David N. Meyer, initially had intended the next album to include songs that would offer listeners an overview of American popular music:

> My original idea for *Sweetheart of the Rodeo* was to do a double, a chronological album, starting with old-timey music—not bluegrass, but pre-bluegrass, dulcimers and Appalachian stuff. Then get into the advanced 1930s version of string music, and move it up to more modern country, the forties and fifties, with pedal steel guitar. Do

the evolution of that kind of music. Then bring it up into electronic music and a kind of space music, and go into futuristic music.

Well, that concept did not last when Gram Parsons passed an audition to become a Byrd. Chris Hillman had known Parsons to be, like himself, a country music devotee. Hillman and Parsons eventually convinced McGuinn that a country recording could succeed.

Guitarist Clarence White was invited to play with other session luminaries—banjoist John Hartford, double bassist Roy Husky, pedal steel guitarist JayDee Maness, and pianist Earl P. Ball. *Sweetheart* includes two Dylan covers, "You Ain't Goin' Nowhere" and "Nothing Was Delivered," and three traditional country numbers, "I Am a Pilgrim," "Blue Canadian Rockies," and "The Christian Life," plus covers of Merle Haggard's "Life in Prison," Luke McDaniel's "You're Still on My Mind," and William Bell's "You Don't Miss Your Water." Woody Guthrie's "Pretty Boy Floyd" and two Parsons compositions, "One Hundred Years from Now" and "Hickory Wind" complete the track listing.

An appearance at Nashville's Grand Old Opry before the album's release was met with boos and heckles from the ultra-conservative audience who objected to having "hippies" perform on so venerable a stage. Ticked off by the spectators' rudeness, Gram Parsons purposely (and famously) sang a song ("Hickory Wind") that was not on the announced list, further distancing the band from the crowd and Opry regulars, including Roy Acuff, on the bill. Born to lead and unperturbed by the fact that McGuinn and Hillman were THE original members of the Byrds and, by extension, held tenure on group decisions, Parsons suggested that the album be billed as performed by "Gram Parsons and the Byrds." Some believe that to lessen Parsons' role on the final production, McGuinn removed Parsons' lead vocals. (They have been restored thankfully.)

For one relatively unknown musician to have assumed a central role in shaping a band's vision so quickly, especially in the case of such an internationally celebrated rock band as the Byrds, remains unprecedented. Parsons' brief but storied time with the Byrds ended with his quitting the band (while in England) on philosophical grounds rather than flying to apartheid South Africa for a performance. Some, however, believe that Parsons' decision was less noble and that he chose to stay put because he wished instead to hang out with new friend Keith Richards.

The Byrds' biggest commercial flop upon its release, a testament to *Sweetheart of the Rodeo*'s greatness has been the respect and adulation it has garnered afterwards. Reviewer Mark Deming, writing for AllMusic, says:

> No major band had gone so deep into the sound and feeling of classic country (without parody or condescension) as the Byrds did on *Sweetheart*; at a time when most rock fans viewed country as a musical "Li'l Abner" routine, the Byrds dared to declare that C&W could be hip, cool, and heartfelt . . . If the Byrds didn't do country music first, they did it brilliantly, and few albums in the style are as beautiful and emotionally affecting as this.

And let there be no doubt about the record's influence on establishing a new genre, country rock, and its prominent progenitors: Brewer & Shipley, The Flying Burrito Brothers, Neil Young, Poco, the Nitty Gritty Dirt Band, Pure Prairie League, and the Eagles.

Artists Who Influenced the Byrds

Bob Dylan, the Beatles, Pete Seeger, the Everly Brothers, the Louvin Brothers, Buck Owens, Chad Mitchell, Gram Parsons, and John Coltrane.

Americana Artists Influenced by the Byrds

Uncle Tupelo, Son Volt, the Jayhawks, Mary Chapin Carpenter, Beachwood Sparks, the Blasters, the Long Ryders, the Nitty Gritty Dirt Band, Wilco, the Silos, Michael Nesmith, Money & King, Tom Petty, and Crazy Horse.

Gram Parsons

"I don't believe anyone would have any interest in me if I'd never met Gram Parsons. He instilled in me a deep love for country music. Before that I was just a Joan Baez wannabe."
(Emmylou Harris)

Roughly thirty years before the Americana Music Association was formed (1999) and forty-plus years before Merriam-Webster included the term "Americana" in the dictionary (2011), Ingram Cecil Connor III, better known as Gram Parsons, had already devised a name for a hybrid of country music that blended R&B, soul, gospel, folk, and rock. He called it: "Cosmic American Music."

As lead vocalist and songwriter of the International Submarine Band, Parsons was chiefly responsible for making the first country-rock album, *Safe at Home* (1968). The groundbreaking *Sweetheart of the Rodeo* (1968) recording simply does not become an iconic LP without Parsons. The Flying Burrito Brothers, which Parsons formed with Chris Hillman in 1968 following their exits from the Byrds, became the most influential country-rock band in history, and its 1969 debut LP, *The Gilded Palace of Sin*, has inspired a who's who list of artists such as Bob Dylan, Emmylou Harris, the Eagles, Keith Richards, Steve Earle, Lucinda Williams, Elvis Costello, Uncle Tupelo, and Dwight Yoakam. Add to this Parsons' solo recordings and you can make a strong case for proclaiming Gram Parsons as Americana's most consequential trailblazer.

Gram Parsons was born in Winter Haven, Florida in 1946 and grew up here and also in Waycross, Georgia, where at age nine, as Jessica Hundley with Polly Parsons write, saw his musical idol, Elvis Presley, on stage:

> Cocky, beautiful, and completely fearless, Elvis threw himself into the performance with a desperate energy . . . Gram watched everything with saucer eyes—the hip shake, the raw ache in that beautiful voice. And he watched the crowd, too. He watched the way the girls' faces had gone pink, mouths slightly open, a slight glint of moisture on the lips. He watched the way they closed their eyes and swayed, the way they clutched the backs of the seats in front of them, knuckles white as they held themselves up, the way the music took hold of them and shook something down deep . . . Later Gram would

> make his way backstage . . . straight into Elvis's dressing room, where he would demand an autograph and offer congratulations with a mix of audacity and good breeding he had learned from his mother.

For the young Bob Dylan, seeing Buddy Holly perform changed everything; for Gram Parsons, it was The King.

In the early 1960s Parsons became a member of the Shilohs, a regionally popular folk group, whose influences included the Kingston Trio and the Journeymen. Besides folk music, the Shilohs, with Parsons contributing originals to the song list, also incorporated bluegrass, gospel, and country blues into their act. However, by 1965, when Dylan and the Byrds had begun electrifying folk, the Shilohs, along with most folk outfits, had trouble generating serious commercial interest. Also, Parsons was, as Bruce Eder points out, "developing interests in country music and rock."

The next step in Parsons' musical journey led to his forming the International Submarine Band in 1965 while studying at Harvard University, where his love of country music took hold with the help of Theology major and future International Submarine Band guitarist, John Nuese, who, as quoted by David N. Meyer, remembers:

> "I started right away to teach him some country music stuff and turned him on to Merle Haggard and Buck Owens. It became apparent to Gram that that was the music that he should be doing. The folk stuff was nice, but it didn't have any *cojones*. Gram knew nothing about what was going on with country music in the sixties and he quickly became an avid fan of the modern country sound, which was Merle Haggard and Buck

Owens. He took on that music and made it his own. He used the time period [September through December of 1965] for his formation of his roots in country music. He learned lots of Haggard and Buck Owens. Those two were the biggest influences on him."

Leaving the Harvard and the Cambridge music scene behind, the International Submarine Band left for New York City in 1966 and then, in 1967, headed to Los Angeles. Parsons settled in Laurel Canyon, home to many of the city's (and the country's) top rock artists: the Byrds, Jim Morrison, Frank Zappa, Love, Joni Mitchell, the Buffalo Springfield, David Crosby, Graham Nash, Eric Burdon, Chris Hillman, Brian Wilson, Jackson Brown, Cass Ellliot, Jimi Hendrix, and Neil Young.

Safe at Home was recorded in December of 1967 but released after the band had broken up. "Born leader" Parsons, only 21 at that time, personified this trait during the session as David N. Meyer states:

> Gram showed a new level of assertiveness, a drive and a sense of ownership over the music. Musically and emotionally, Gram was a collaborator only to a degree. After years of wanting the spotlight, he did not waste his opportunity. Patterns were established that would hold true in all his recording sessions: a distaste for structuring his material before going into the studio; a preference for playing live with the tape machine running; not much interest in listening to a producer; ruthless about finding the best player for the part, regardless of whose feelings might get hurt; and a sense that everyone was laboring in the service of his vision.

But Meyer applauds the result:

> In fairness, Gram drove himself to a standard that made it reasonable for him to be ruthless with others. At first listen, an outstanding aspect of *Safe at Home* is the skill with which the band apes then-current and traditional honky-tonk forms. To seek to capture those forms was a revolutionary, not evolutionary, step in 1967. There were no longhair rockers exploring sounds with Gram's accuracy and attention to detail or his fealty to the cultural mythology underlying the music. The album is pure City of Industry honky-tonk, executed with loving gusto and hell-raising sincerity, even on the joke songs.

Safe at Home includes four Parsons originals: "Blue Eyes," "Luxury Liner," "Strong Boy," and "Do You Know How It Feels to Be Lonesome" (co-written with Barry Goldberg). A Johnny Cash/Elvis Presley medley, "Folsom Prison Blues/That's All Right," Cash's "I Still Miss Someone," and Merle Haggard's "I Must Be Somebody Else You've Known" are other notable tracks. At the time of its release the album did not even crack the *Billboard* 200. Country music, even played by young, spirited long-hairs, seemed anachronistic, out-of-step with the times and not relatable to the youth culture. As Roger McGuinn, as quoted by Meyer, mentions: "Our [the Byrds'] fans were heartbroken that we'd sold out to the enemy. Politically, country music represented the right-wing redneck people who liked guns. We were the pioneers—with arrows in our backs." But history would prove to be on the side of these trailblazers. The great risks taken by Bob Dylan, the Byrds, and Gram Parsons to satisfy their musical ethos established their status as rock and roll hierarchy.

To more fully explore the Cosmic American musical terrain begun with the International Submarine Band and the Byrds, Parsons and recently flown Byrd, Chris Hillman, in 1968 formed the seminal country-rock band, The Flying Burrito Bothers. Bassist Chris Ethridge and drummer Jon Corneal from the International Submarine Band, along with pedal steel guitarist "Sneaky Pete" Kleinow, rounded out the group. The 1969 release of *The Gilded Palace of Sin* enjoyed critical acclaim and memorable artwork that featured front and back photos of the band wearing custom sequin outfits from designer Nudie Cohn, called Nudie suits. Parsons' suit displayed a naked woman, red poppies, and marijuana leaves. Though it only reached #164 on *Billboard*, the recording has, over time, secured the #1 spot in the hearts and minds of country-rock devotees.

The Gilded Palace of Sin was Bob Dylan's favorite country-rock album, saying (from telegraph.com) that the LP "instantly knocked me out" Mark Deming in his review believes that on this record Parsons "revealed the full extent of his talents, and it ranks among the finest and most influential albums the genre would ever produce." Perhaps no rock critic has articulated the greatness of this debut album as perceptively as has writer Bob Proehl:

> Its blend of country, rock, psychedelia and R&B failed to find a large audience, but its influence stretched throughout the country rock movement of the '70s and laid in wait behind the commercial success of bands like the Eagles, waiting to be discovered by a new generation of rockers who would spearhead the alt-country movement in the late '80s and early '90s. The Burrito Brothers' ability to fuse disparate musical elements encouraged these bands, many of them raised on a combination of country and punk, to go back

to the roots of country music and find its still-beating heart, buried under the shellac of commercial country.

The Gilded Palace of Sin is also a superb example of Americana music as Proehl (above) proves.

Nine of the eleven tracks are originals by Parsons with either Hillman, Ethridge, or Goldberg as co-writers. "Do Right Woman" and "Dark End of the Street" are the two covers. Although Parsons sings most of the leads, the majority of the songs feature the soulful, Everly Brothers-like harmonies of Parsons and Hillman. The effect of Parsons' cracked, weathered, and heartfelt voice with the smooth, softly textured tones from Hillman on the listener is palpable. Parsons plays acoustic guitar, piano, and organ; Hillman, acoustic guitar and mandolin. And Kleinow provides sounds never heard before or since on the pedal steel. The fresh combination of these musical ingredients inspired Farmer Dave from the band Beachwood Sparks when he spoke to author Jessica Hundley:

> Sneaky Pete Kleinow, with his fuzz/delayed pedaled approach to the instrument, was one of my favorite musicians right off the bat. When I'd hear the way his notes bounced and flew all around the band and Gram Parsons' voice in "Dark End of the Street," I'd feel like I was in a hot tub after having some good tequila. I ended up joining up with the fellows and starting Beachwood Sparks. Gram Parsons and his legacy were a cornerstone foundation of our style at the start, and we wore it on our sleeves, literally, with the vintage western shirts, long hair, and recreational habits.

The next Flying Burrito Brothers album, *Burrito Deluxe* (1970) would be Gram Parsons' last with the band. As was the case with his brief tenure in the Byrds, Parsons' desire to be with the Rolling Stones, specifically with Keith Richards, rather than dedicating more time with the Burritos, led to his dismissal following the record's release. Though his friendship with Richards certainly intensified Parsons' drug and alcohol dependency, artistically the relationship proved valuable for Richards as he describes in *Life*:

> Gram taught me country music—how it worked, the difference between the Bakersfield style and the Nashville style . . . I learned the piano from Gram and started writing songs on it. Some of the seeds he planted in the country music area are still with me . . . I know I've had a good teacher . . . Of all the musicians I know personally (although Otis Redding, who I didn't know, fits this too), the two who had an attitude that was the same as mine were Gram Parsons and John Lennon . . . Gram was a bold man. This guy never had a hit record. Some good sellers, but nothing to point to, yet his influence is stronger now than ever. Basically, you wouldn't have had Waylon Jennings, you wouldn't have had all that outlaw movement without Gram Parsons. He showed them a new approach, that country music isn't just a narrow thing that appeals to rednecks.

Parsons' relationship with Richards extended to his presence at the recording sessions of *Exile on Main Street*, the Rolling Stones' most critically-acclaimed album. David N. Meyer points out that "there's no proof that Gram directly participated in any songs on *Exile*, but the influence of his taste and philosophy is everywhere."

The second Burrito album saw former Byrd Michael Clarke taking over drum duties and Bernie Leadon, future member of the Eagles, playing lead guitar, dobro, and adding vocals. Leadon also penned "God's Own Singer" and co-wrote three other tracks. Parsons resurrected his composition "Lazy Days" from his days with the Byrds and with Hillman and/or Leadon authored five more tunes. Two of the four covers worth noting are Bob Dylan's "If You Gotta Go" and the Jaggers/Richards hit "Wild Horses." Its appearance on this album actually precedes by a year its release by the Rolling Stones. Some conjecture that Gram Parsons actually wrote the song.

A sampling of the artists who have covered songs from *The Gilded Palace of Sin* and *Burrito Deluxe* speaks to its transcendent powers: Dwight Yoakam & k.d. lang, Uncle Tupelo, Beck & Emmylou Harris ("Sin City"); Elvis Costello, the Mavericks ("Hot Burrito #1"); Sheryl Crow and Emmylou Harris ("Juanita"); Emmylou Harris ("Wheels"); Willie Nelson ("Do Right Woman"); Richard and Linda Thompson, Linda Ronstadt ("Dark End Of the Street"); Chris Hillman and Steve Earle ("High Fashion Queen"); Rolling Stones ("Wild Horses"); Tom Petty and the Heartbreakers ("Image of Me"); Dolly Parton, Emmylou Harris, and Linda Ronstadt ("Farther Along''). (The interpretations of the non-original Burrito songs listed above are closer to the Burrito versions.)

Before going any further into Parsons' story, special attention must be given to his sidekick Chris Hillman, without whom Parsons would not have joined the Byrds or formed the Flying Burrito Brothers. The unassuming and multi-talented Hillman ultimately became a critical member of the Byrds, helping the band incorporate country music into their songs. In retrospect, Hillman's importance to the Byrds, country rock, and Americana continues to gain momentum. Following the Burritos, Hillman played in Manassas, the Souther Hillman Furay Band, McGuinn, Clark & Hillman, and the Desert Rose Band, in addition to his recordings with Herb Pedersen. In an interview with Lee Zimmerman, who refers to Hillman as the "Americana Godfather," Hillman recalls his tenure with Parsons and the Burritos: "The first year was really good. Then we lost him. We lost him to excess, and I had to part company with him. I just remember the good times. He was funny. He was bright. He was great to write songs with. He had a great take on things."

Although calling *Burrito Deluxe* "certainly a better than average country-rock album," reviewer Mark Deming says that "coming from a band who made the genre's most strongly defining music, it's something of a disappointment." Deming notes that unlike the previous albums where Parsons "became the focal point, regardless of the talents of his compatriots . . . he seems to have deliberately stepped back to make more room for others." However, with his next two albums, *GP* (1973) and *Grievous Angel* (1974), Gram Parsons flies solo.

It had been close to three years since Gram Parsons' last recording when he began *GP*. Initially, his idol Merle Haggard had agreed to produce the record, but the arrangement fell through. Parsons did at least secure the services of Haggard's engineer, Hugh Davies, and former Blind Faith bassist, Ric Grech, as producer. The musicians backing Parsons featured Elvis Presley's band: James Burton/guitar, Glen D. Hardin/piano and organ, and Ronnie Tut/drums. Renowned fiddle player Byron Berline and highly sought-after pedal steel guitarists Al Perkins and Buddy Emmons were also hired. The most consequential invitee to the sessions was the addition of an unknown singer working in Washington D.C. whom Parsons had recently discovered (with Chris Hillman's assistance), Emmylou

Harris, whose spellbinding harmonies with Parsons would become legendary.

GP did not make Gram Parsons a lot of money or make him famous. The album and its single "She" did not appear on *Billboard* 200, and Parsons would not be a familiar name until years later. But critics, musicians, and (later) more and more listeners became smitten with the soulful, bluesy, tear-producing, passionate renderings of original and traditional country numbers. These nuggets from Bud Scoppa, writing for *Rolling Stone* in March of 1973, reflect the enthusiasm of many reviewers:

> Gram Parsons is an artist with a vision as unique and personal as those of Jaggers-Richards, Ray Davies . . . The album is just what Gram's devotees have been waiting for . . . Together, Gram and Emmylou form a duo that's right up there with George-Tammy and Conway-Loretta in style, but with the added principal of moral uncertainty . . . The other important dimension is the innuendo supplied by Gram's voice and delivery. He may not be old enough to be a Haggard or a Cash, but he gets another kind of worldliness, a quieter kind of strength out of his singing. That amazing voice with its warring qualities of sweetness and dissipation . . .

Like his previous recordings with the International Submarine Band, the Byrds, and the Flying Burrito Brothers, Parsons offers a number of originals: "Still Feeling Blue," "A Song for You," "She," "The New Soft Show," "How Much I've Lied," and "Big Mouth Blues" which have been covered by the likes of Kasey Chambers, Whiskeytown, Norah Jones, the Pretenders, and Elvis Costello. Though unlike the other albums, Parsons' song selection reflects more the Nashville rather than Bakersfield sound with his covers of "That's All It Took" (Darrell Edwards, Charlotte Grier, George Jones) and "We'll Sweep Out the Ashes in the Morning" (Joyce Allsup). Parsons also covers the outlaw-country "Streets of Baltimore" (Tompall Glaser, Harlan Howard) and the J. Geils Band's R&B number "Cry One More Time" (Peter Wolf, Seth Justman).

Gram Parsons did not live to see the release of his final album, *Grievous Angel*. He had died from a morphine/alcohol overdose four months earlier at the much-too-early age of 26. As with his recent solo effort, the recording sessions were made more difficult by Parsons' often failed efforts at remaining sober. Somehow Parsons and company worked through his demons and produced what has come down to be called Parsons' Cosmic American masterpiece. The studio personnel remained basically the same except for the presence of Bernie Leadon and brief appearances of Herb Pederson and Linda Ronstadt.

Of the nine cuts, six are composed by Parsons, of which the two most regarded were written alone: "Brass Buttons" and "$1000 Wedding." A live medley includes a song Parsons recorded with the Byrds, "Hickory Wind," and a rousing, foot-stomping cover of the Louvin Brothers' "Cash on the Barrelhead." The heartfelt Parsons/Harris duets ("Heart of Fire," "Love Hurts,") have never been surpassed. And "I Can't Dance" and "Ooh Las Vegas" validate how Parsons combines country with rock like no else.

The two most autobiographical songs, "The Return of the Grievous Angel" and "In My Hour of Darkness," lyrically and emotionally elevate Parsons' stature among songwriters, as Emmylou Harris said to interviewer Nigel Williamson from the Hundley/Parsons biography: "He [Gram] was an innovator and he came up with something completely different. He was the first person who brought rock poetry to country music." Speaking to interviewer

Steve Wosahla, popular Americana musician Jim Lauderdale calls *Grievous Angel* his favorite album: "It knew I could never duplicate *Grievous Angel*, but it set a bar to aspire to. It still sounds fresh. It's a perfect record in every way."

Although many claim that Gram Parsons founded country rock, he hated the term and particularly a group most often associated with the genre, the Eagles, whose music he derided as "plastic dry-fuck." Despite the fact that former bandmate and friend Bernie Leadon was an Eagle, who after Parsons' death would compose a touching song ("My Man") in his memory, author David M. Meyer attempts to interpret Parsons' animosity:

> Eagles' drummer Don Henley said of himself: "I have a high tolerance for repetition." Gram lacked this quality. Henley's abundance of it helped provide the Eagles with its soulless, over-rehearsed, antiseptic, schematic, insincere, sentimental core. The Eagles managed to deny every roots-music source of their sound. Their country rock—with its self-satisfaction, misogyny, absence of pain, junior high emotions, pop hooks, and facile virtuosity—was more than dumb enough to please the broadest American audience . . . He [Gram] bore the Eagles a special loathing as any sane listener might.

The Hank Williams of his generation, declared Bob Dylan. "An enduring musical force. He's like a tributary, or a stream, coming from a place all his own, but part of a larger musical tradition," observed Farmer Dave. Father of "the transcendental mix of the jambalaya of rock, soul, country, gospel, and blues" that he christened "Cosmic American

Music" (and that today is called "Americana") confirms biographer David N. Meyer. Gram Parsons was all of the above and much more. The following assessment from journalist Nathan Rabin expresses Parsons' legacy quite well:

> Gram Parsons has a decidedly mixed reputation as a country artist for people who don't like country music. With his pouty, androgynous good looks, privileged background, inveterate hipness, folkie past, and rock-star pals, Parsons defied the stereotype of country singers as backward hillbillies, but there was nothing ironic or post-modern about Parsons' approach to country, especially as a solo artist. Parsons wasn't goofing on country or subverting its conventions; he genuinely loved the genre, its hardscrabble roots, and working-class soul. Parsons worshipped unabashedly at the altar of George Jones and Merle Haggard, even if the country establishment had no use for him. In his lifetime, Parsons was stuck between worlds. He was too country for hippies and the Sunset Strip cool kids, but way too hippie and rock 'n' roll for the country crowd . . . But Parsons' legend has flourished posthumously. Though a non-entity commercially over the course of his lifetime, Parsons inspired a generation of artists in multiple genres and became the preeminent martyr of the alt-country movement. He is a quintessential cult artist, relatively forgotten in his lifetime, yet a pioneer and creative giant in death.

Artists Who Influenced Gram Parsons

Buck Owens, Merle Haggard, Bob Dylan, Elvis Presley, the Beatles, Hank Williams, Woody Guthrie, Buddy Holly, the Louvin Brothers, Johnny Cash, Tom Paxton, and the Everly Brothers.

Americana Artists Influenced by Gram Parsons

Son Volt, Beachwood Sparks, Ryan Adams, Jimmie Dale Gilmore, Rosanne Cash, Emmylou Harris, Gillian Welch, Joe Ely, the Jayhawks, Jim Lauderdale, Lucinda Williams, Steve Earle, Uncle Tupelo, Wilco, Alejandro Escovedo, Waco Brothers, the Felice Brothers, the Long Ryders, the Blasters, Maria McKee, Ass Ponys, the Coal Porters, Blue Rodeo, and Jason & the Scorchers.

Gene Clark

"We [The Byrds] learned a lot of
songwriting from him and in the process
learned a little bit about ourselves."
(Chris Hillman)

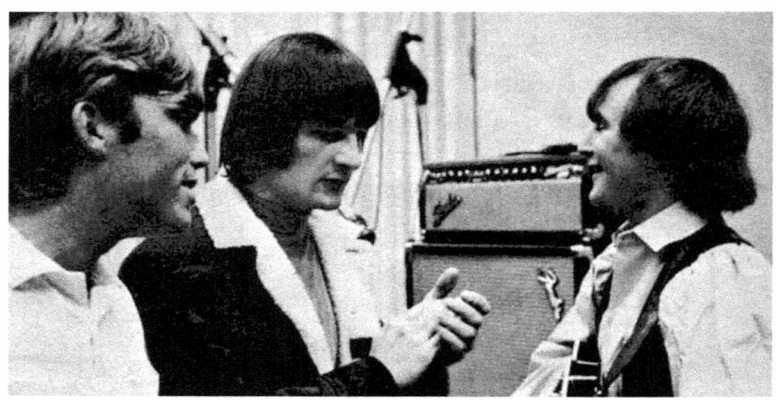

Of all Americana's trailblazers, the artist who has earned the least recognition for his contributions to this genre is Gene Clark. Founding member and chief songwriter of the Byrds, Clark, who after leaving the Byrds produced two of the earliest and finest country-rock albums—*Gene Clark with the Gosdin Brothers* (1967) and *The Fantastic Expedition of Dillard and Clark* (1968), and two quintessential Americana releases—*White Light* (1971) and *No Other* (1974), like fellow pathfinder Gram Parsons, would not be fully appreciated for his genre-bending prowess and sublime songwriting until well past his death at age 46 in 1991.

As was typical of his musical contemporaries and future bandmates, Gene Clark's early influences included rockers (Elvis Presley) and folk singers (the Kingston Trio). He also demonstrated a fondness for Hank Williams. Following his stint with two Kansas City folk groups, the Rum Runners and the Surf Riders, in 1963 at age 19 he was invited to join the New Christy Minstrels, the most popular American large-ensemble folk group of the era. After recording two albums with the Minstrels, Clark moved to Los Angeles in 1964 where, at the Troubadour Club, he met Roger McGuinn and David Crosby and together would form the Byrds.

Gene Clark was a critical member of the Byrds, offering his rich tenor or baritone to both lead and background vocals but, more importantly, sharing his songwriting gifts as composer of "I'll Feel a Whole Lot Better," "She Don't Care About Time," "Here Without You," "Set You Free This Time," and "Eight Miles High." Clark's presence on stage with the Byrds was also something to behold as Chris Hillman relates to Randy Lewis of *The Los Angeles Times*: "At one time, he was the power in the Byrds, not McGuinn, not Crosby—it was Gene who burst through the stage curtain banging on a tambourine, coming on like a young Prince Valiant."

Wishing to pursue his own musical vision, following his flight from the Byrds in 1966, Gene Clark proceeded to enlist the help of the Gosdin Brothers, originally known as the Hillmen, a southern California bluegrass band formed in 1962. Chris Hillman had played mandolin in this group before his tenure with the Byrds, so Clark already had a connection with the band. Vern Gosdin, who later rolled out a string of top 10 hits on the country music charts, furnished backing vocals with brother Rex. Assisting Clark and the Gosdins in the studio were these luminaries—Glen Campbell and Clarence White on electric guitars, Doug Dillard on electric banjo, Leon Russell on piano and harpsichord, Jim Gordon and Michael Clarke on drums, Van Dyke Parks on keyboards, and Chris Hillman on bass. The stitching together of these assorted threads in the production of *Gene Clark with the Gosdin Brothers* was revolutionary. Clark proved that bluegrass, country rock, folk rock, and baroque rock could be woven to create a unique musical quilt.

Byrds-style songs ("Couldn't Believe Her," "The Same One," "So You Say You Lost Your Baby"), Beatlesesque tracks ("Elevator Operator," "Is Yours Is Mine"), and bluegrass/country-inspired cuts ("Keep on Pushin'" "Tried So Hard,"—a tune that Fairport Convention, the Flying Burrito Brothers, and Yo La Tengo would cover) testify to Clark's original grasp of various musical expressions. Reviewer Michael Fremer has this to say about the album:

> This resourceful, pioneering album is anything but "of a genre," though it includes elements of country rock, before there was such a category. The album is original, experimental and daring . . . and showcases Clark's compositional and rhythmic sophistication, and his singular melodic gift . . . his burning originality punches through the malleable musical settings . . . And then there's the melancholic voice; the aching catch, and the deep yearning and sadness that runs through nearly all of the material Clark wrote and sang throughout his long but unfulfilled career. It's a pure, honest voice one never tires of hearing because Clark communicated deftly and daringly from a place of pure vulnerability. Cushioning Clark are backing harmonies influenced by The

Everlys, The Beatles, The Mamas and the Papas and others.

A year later (1968), Clark released an album considered by many as the first progressive bluegrass recording as well as a country-rock masterpiece, *The Fantastic Expedition of Dillard & Clark*. Before teaming with Clark, banjoist extraordinaire Doug Dillard had played in two renowned bluegrass bands, the Ozark Mountain Boys and the Dixie Ramblers, a group which featured fiddle and banjo virtuoso John Hartford, and the Dillards, who found a national following for their (1963-1966) recurring role on TV's *The Andy Griffith Show* as the Darlings of Mayberry bluegrass outfit. Dillard, who was among those musicians guesting on Clark's previous solo effort, helped compose seven of the nine tunes. Future Flying Burrito Brother and Eagle, Bernie Leadon, contributed banjo and guitar while co-writing six of the nine songs on the record, and, on two tracks, Chris Hillman picked his mandolin. Only one cover appeared on the LP, Lester Flatt and Earl Scruggs and The Foggy Mountain Boys' hit "Get In Line Brother" (rephrased as "Get It On Brother").

Doug Dillard also played fiddle, an instrument that increasingly found expanded roles with Americana's trailblazers. The list of fiddle players who recorded with these pioneers includes these masters: Byron Berline (Bob Dylan, the Band, the Byrds, Gram Parsons, Gene Clark), John Hartford (the Byrds, Gene Clark), Vassar Clements (the Grateful Dead) and Gib Guilbeau (Arlo Guthrie). Berline and Guilbeau would become members of the post-Parsons Flying Burrito Brothers. Their influence extends to current Americana fiddle favorites Mark O'Connor, Allison Krauss, Stuart Duncan, Michael Cleveland, and Natalie MacMaster.

The album's importance in adding bluegrass elements to other musical styles laid the foundation for what later would be termed "progressive bluegrass." Progressive bluegrass is a sub-genre of Americana that incorporates folk, country, rock, jazz, and/or blues into an amplified bluegrass foundation. Some celebrated Americana progressive bluegrass artists who exemplify what Dillard & Clark explored include Allison Krauss & Union Station, Bela Fleck, Jerry Douglas, New Grass Revival, Trampled by Turtles, Yonder Mountain String Band, the Seldom Scene, the Del McCoury Band, Sam Bush, Tony Rice, Hot Rize, and Tim O'Brien. The progressive bluegrass sound of *The Fantastic Expedition of Dillard & Clark* is also echoed in the music of Neil Young, John Prine, Iris DeMent, Guy Clark, Lyle Lovett, Dwight Yoakam, and Fleet Foxes.

Gene Clark's songwriting with the Byrds and his first solo album had earned much respect, but with the latest release came much praise. From the *Los Angeles Times* music blog, "Pop & Hiss":

> The first track, "Out on the Side," [is] a floating Clark-penned classic featuring glorious vocal harmonies, Dillard and Clark's tangled guitar and banjo conversation, and rich, humming organ adding texture below . . . Fans of country & western, alternative country or any combination thereof will find much to love on the album. There's twang galore, but it's a smooth, casual kind, mixed with acoustic strums, loaming bass lines and stunning harmonies.

From Therisingstorm.net, commentaries on the next tracks:

> A lush and laid-back troupe owns it on "She Darked the Sun," setting the tone firmly, nailed down by the straight-up Dillards feel

on "Don't Come Rolling." The "Gene Clark" sound takes it back for the next few songs: a triumvirate of gems molding the sweet spot of the record and providing all the proof we need to declare this a legendary matchup . . . *Fantastic Expedition* grows better and better, undoubtedly with each listen. It is pure joy, pure beauty, a one of a kind favorite and sort of a miracle for the genres of both rock and country.

As was the case with the Byrds, Gene Clark's fears of flying and performing in front of a live audience drastically hindered record sales. Panic-attack episodes haunted Clark throughout his life and severely impacted commercial sales of his recordings. Johnny Rogan, author of an exhaustive Byrds biography, writing in the *Irish Times* believes that two events in Clark's childhood (from which he never fully recovered) contributed mightily to lifelong anxiety issues: being trapped inside a church as a tornado moved through his hometown in Missouri and witnessing a deadly private plane crash. Rogan suggests that along with inheriting a propensity for alcohol from his Irish-Catholic, Native-American lineage, the psychological obstacles only fueled his desire for drink as a means of escape. Ultimately, extreme alcohol consumption over a period of years would shorten his life.

Rogan, more positively, explains how Clark's Irish Catholic roots influenced his songwriting:

> Clark's best work is full of imagination. His songs include references to eternity, angels and souls, while many of his love ballads dramatize a moral complexity, with protestations of guilt, remorse and the need for forgiveness. Even an innocuously titled

> song such as "So You Say You Lost Your Baby" contains some fantastical imagery and casually conceived cosmological concepts . . . the symbolism and complex imagery resonate with each fresh listening and much of it can clearly be traced back to his childhood education when the Catechism addressed profound questions of theology with the simple conviction and authority of an instruction manual.

Gene Clark, like fellow trailblazer Bob Dylan, is both singer and poet. Along with the blending of genres in the construction of a song, another vital feature distinguishing Americana from mainstream music is the emphasis placed on the value of words—the memorable phrase, the original figure of speech, the startling image, the insightful remark, and the heartfelt expression.

Dillard & Clark hooked up for another progressive bluegrass, country-rock album, *Through the Morning, Through the Night* (1969) with a few personnel changes from the previous record. Most notably were the additions of Sneaky Pete Kleinow (pedal steel guitar), Byron Berline (fiddle), Jon Corneal (drums), and Donna Washburn (vocals). Gene Clark's songwriting takes a backseat to an LP replete with bluegrass covers: "No Longer a Sweetheart of Mine," "Rocky Top," "I Bowed My Head and Cried Holy," and "Roll in My Sweet Baby's Arms." Dillard & Clark also offer versions of the Everly Brothers' "So Sad" and the Beatles' "Don't Let Me Down."

Clark did, however, manage to compose four songs on the release—"Through the Morning, Through the Night," "Corner Street Bar," "Kansas City Southern," and "Polly." Robert Plant & Alison Kraus beautifully covered "Through the Morning, Through the Night" and "Polly" (retitled "Polly Come Home") on their much-acclaimed *Raising*

Sand album. The autobiographical "Kansas City Southern" poignantly evokes Clark's memories of the trains that rolled down the track near his home. Sneaky Pete's pedal steel playing is a marvel on this cut as his instrument simulates the Southern's movements, and Clark's voice captures both the excitement and lonesomeness that the train's passing renders. Frustrated by the poor record sales and the negative reviews of the Dillard & Clark follow-up, Gene Clark chose to leave the band.

  One notable, albeit peculiar, exception to the dearth of record sales with his solo albums and the Dillard & Clark effort was Clark's second, *White Light* (1971), which was only released in the Netherlands and where it was voted album of the year. With two members of the Steve Miller Band, drummer Gary Mallader and pianist Ben Sidran, and former Burrito Brother bassist Chris Ethridge assisting, Clark, according to reviewer Thom Jurek, made "one of the greatest singer/songwriter albums ever made." Jurek continues: "Using melodies mutated out of country, and revealing that he was the original poet and architect of the Byrds sound, Clark created a wide open set of tracks that are at once full of space, a rugged gentility, and are harrowingly intimate in places."

  Only one of the nine songs, Bob Dylan and Richard Manuel's "Tears of Rage," is not written by Gene Clark. Speaking of Dylan, producer Jesse Ed Davis, who also played electric guitar, and engineers Joe Zagarino and Baker Bigsby, wrapped most of the songs in skeletal, *John Wesley Harding*-style arrangements with few vocal harmonies. The result is a recording that "proves beyond any doubt that Clark was the strongest singer of the legendary band [the Byrds]," asserts writer Jason Heller, adding that "throughout *White Light*, Clark's lush, haunting baritone fills every empty corner of the songs." More praise for the LP comes from Therisingstorm.net: "This is good American roots music in a style only Gene owned . . . Regardless of classification, the tunes are downright beautiful, and incredibly original."

Several of Gene Clark's greatest songs—"White Light," "With Tomorrow," "Because of You," "One in a Hundred," "For a Spanish Guitar," and "Where My Love Lies Asleep"—bear witness to the *White Light's* transcendence.

Following the release of *Roadmaster* (1973), a superb compilation of unreleased recordings initially released in the Netherlands and Germany, Clark returned to the studio and delivered what many judge as his magnum opus, *No Other* (1974). Another commercial failure at the time of its release, the LP, nonetheless, continues to attract legions of appreciative listeners. Thom Jurek, reviewing the album for AllMusic, describes the LP as "a sprawling, ambitious work that brought elements of country, folk, jazzed-out gospel, blues, and trippy rock to bear on a song cycle that reflects the mid-'70s better than anything from that time, yet sounds hauntingly timely even now." This was, in many ways, Gene Clark's *White Album*.

Clark recruited an amazing array of talented musicians including Chris Hillman (mandolin), Danny Kortchmar (guitar), Joe Lala (percussion), Lee Sklar (bass), and Butch Trucks (drums). Apparently Sly Stone visited some sessions to lend his expertise on the R&B cuts. The production is unlike anything found on Clark's other recordings as the Phil Spector/Brian Wilson-sounding arrangements, saturated with overdubbing and sophisticated harmonies, attest.

All nine songs on the album were written by Gene Clark with the exception of "Lady of the North" which he wrote with Doug Dillard, with whom he hadn't recorded since 1969. Perhaps no other trailblazer came as close to displaying the art and range of musical genre-bending as did Gene Clark on *No Other*. Of more consequence, of course, are the magnificent songs that he crafted within the context of the multi-genre structure.

Side one starts off with "Life's Greatest Fool," a country-rock lament on man's daily walk with paradox; next up, "Silver Raven," another country rocker, adds gospel backup vocals. A psychedelic funk number, "No Other," the third track, is followed by "Strength of Strings," which could be labeled psychedelic blues. Track #1 on side two is a song which is more pop than country in melody and features several anti-drug messages among its enigmatic lyrics. "Some Misunderstanding," the next cut, fuses the sounds of country, rock, blues, and gospel with introspective words. A true country song, "True One," and the ethereal "Lady of the North," which blends R&B, electric blues, Celtic folk, and psychedelia, completes the iconoclastic and delectable musical feast.

Gene Clark would record three more albums, his last a collaboration with Carla Olson, the well-received *So Rebellious a Lover* (1987), before his death brought on by a bleeding ulcer in 1991. His legacy, however, lives on. In 2013 the documentary film *The Byrd Who Flew Alone: The Triumphs and Tragedy of Gene Clark* received great reviews. In 2014 a group of indie musicians got together and toured the U.S. playing *No Other*. *Gene Clark—The Lost Studio Session, 1964-1982* was released to much praise in 2016 with more collections of unreleased material to be made available soon. Recently, re-releases of *No Other* and *White Light* have also appeared.

Michael Clarke, close friend and bandmate, paid tribute to Gene Clark at the time of Clark's death in this excerpt from *Full Circle* magazine:

> Gene and I were quite close. For 21 years he was like a brother to me. I only have a few words I wish to say. Gene was an artist, a true expressionist. Expression is man's potent

instrument of progress. His success is inevitably measured or limited by his ability to communicate his thoughts to others. Gene Clark was one of the most successful and loving people I ever met. A continuous battle raged between Gene and himself, which in the end found its way onto paper and into song, where it settled. He was never bothered with the trendy-or-popular, for-the-moment type of music. His style was never inimical, but limitless and different. In my opinion Gene Clark has earned, along with all the other folk heroes, a seat in the "Folk Heroes Hall of Fame" and a permanent place in all our hearts.

Artists Who Influenced Gene Clark

Bob Dylan, the New Christy Minstrels, the Louvin Brothers, the Stanley Brothers, Hank Williams, Tom Paxton, Jimmie Rodgers, Bill Monroe, and Phil Ochs.

Americana Artists Influenced by Gene Clark

Tom Petty, Chris Hillman, Alejandro Escovedo, Son Volt, the Textones, the Long Ryders, and Lambchop.

Buffalo Springfield

"Once you decide that it is the art that is important and not how popular and well received you are, you no longer have an albatross."
(Stephen Stills)

That three of the five original members of the short-lived (1966-1968) yet storied band Buffalo Springfield were Canadian appears ironic today when discussing the group in the framework of Americana music. Of course, the genre by this name refers only to the American roots-based musical elements in the sound, not to the places of birth of its performers. (The Americana Music Association, for example, has official partnerships in the United Kingdom and Australia.) What is of more consequence, certainly, is how Canadians Dewey Martin (drums, vocals), Bruce Palmer (bass), and Neil Young (guitar, piano, harmonica, vocals) united with Americans Richie Furay (guitar, vocals) and Stephen Stills (guitar, keyboards, vocals) and established what many consider as the greatest rock band of its era, if not its most influential.

Once again, Los Angeles (and Laurel Canyon) proved to be the ideal place for Americana's pioneers to pitch camp while blazing their musical trails. Just as David Crosby, Roger McGuinn and Gene Clark were fated to meet at the Troubadour in 1964, destiny intervened with another set of musicians in 1966 as Justin Joffe narrates:

> When Young drove West from Toronto with fellow Canadian and certified roustabout Bruce Palmer, he'd already cut his teeth playing with Stephen Stills back at Fort Williams in Thunder Bay, Ontario. He knew Stills had moved out to L.A. from New York first, but had no idea where. And it was a traffic jam that finally brought Buffalo Springfield together . . . Stills was driving with Richie Furay in a white van when they got stuck in traffic on Sunset Boulevard. Shooing a fly off his arm, Furay saw in his peripheral a black hearse with Ontario plates traveling in the other direction, and immediately knew who it was [Young] . . . He and Palmer were actually on their way to San Francisco when Stills and Furay found them.

After adopting the name of an American steamroller brand, "Buffalo Springfield," and following their debut at the

Troubadour and a tour as the opening act for the Dillards and the Byrds, the Canadian-American band played a rousing six-week, house-band stand at the Whisky a Go Go. Interestingly, the audition to play at the Whisky was initiated by Chris Hillman of the Byrds, a rival band of sorts. The success of the Whisky shows led to a recording contract and the release of *Buffalo Springfield* in late 1966.

From the re-issued album (1967) came one of rock history's most famous protest songs and Buffalo Springfield's biggest hit, "For What It's Worth," written by Stephen Stills. The song was a response to the 1966 Sunset Strip curfew riots where police and hippies clashed. Other songs of note include "Go and Say Goodbye," "Sit Down, I Think I Love You," and "Nowadays Clancy Can't Even Sing." Pop, folk-rock and country-rock styles are heavily featured on the recordings. All twelve songs are original compositions from Stephen Stills (7) and Neil Young (5) with Stills and Richie Furay dominating the vocals. In fact, Young only sings lead on two tracks ("Burned" and "Out of Mind"). Right from the group's founding it was apparent which two members would lead the band.

Although not fully realized until the next release, *Buffalo Springfield Again* (1967), what differentiated Buffalo Springfield from their contemporaries and marked their inheritance to later rock bands were the dynamic guitar work from Stills and Young, the creative songwriting, and the awe-inspiring harmonies. Added to these features is a flair for cohesively combining a variety of musical genres as the second album confirms. A listener can detect not only folk rock ("Bluebird") and country rock ("A Child's Claim to Fame") but also R&B ("Good Time Boy"), jazz ("Everydays"), hard rock ("Mr. Soul") and psychedelic rock ("Expecting to Fly"). The song credits for the ten tracks on *Buffalo Springfield Again* belong to Stephen Stills (4), Neil Young (3), and Richie Furay (3).

Buffalo Springfield, like the Byrds and Flying Burrito Brothers, had their share of personnel exiting and entering the band. Neil Young, who would quit the band three times in two years, took a leave of absence prior to the Monterey Pop Festival gig, and David Crosby was recruited to take his spot on stage. Bassist Bruce Palmer was deported to Canada twice for drug possession and later replaced by Jim Messina of future Loggins & Messina fame. And a number of drummers occasionally sat in for Dewey Martin on the last two studio albums, *Buffalo Springfield Again* (1968) and *Last Time Around* (1968).

The major internal conflict that led to the group's breakup in 1968, however, was the steady tension between Stephen Stills and Neil Young. Each of the two born leaders refused to play second fiddle to the other. Gavin Martin explains:

> In *Spinal Tap* terms, Furay was the mild-mannered element, sandwiched between Young's ice-cold calculation and Stills' fiery creativity . . . "It was Steve's Band: he was the inspiration, the motivator and the heart and soul. I saw both of them as tremendously talented; I was happy to play my part," says Furay. "I think early on we all saw our individual roles, and those roles weren't intimidating or threatening. The unfortunate thing was, it didn't continue." Nicknamed The General because of his military background and habit of taking control, Stills was a wildly ambitious figure. By his 20th birthday he'd lived in three continents, soaking up everything from deep blues, Gregorian chants and Latin American rhythms . . . "The fact I was the leader of the band was probably what led to its demise,

Neil Young not being the type to be led," Stills cackles.

Whatever differences Stills and Young shared did not prevent the two from their illustrious collaborations in Buffalo Springfield and later with Crosby, Stills, Nash & Young and the Stills-Young Band. Both men, then and now, have remained friends and fierce admirers of the other person's musical gifts.

An excellent farewell album (and title), *Last Time Around*, once more showcased Buffalo Springfield's original and incomparable songwriting, singing, and playing. Two of Young's best known compositions, "I Am a Child" and "On the Way Home," and Stills' Latin-inspired "Pretty Girl Why" and "Uno Mundo," are highlights, but the heretofore underrated talents of Richie Furay sparkle as writer and lead singer on "In the Hour of Not Quite Rain" and (especially) "Kind Woman," which he would perform regularly with Poco or as a solo act. Furay's sweet, clear tenor, as lead vocalist or harmonizer, imparted as much to the "Springfield sound" as did the guitar virtuosity of Stills and Young.

In 2010 the surviving members of Buffalo Springfield—Stephen Stills, Neil Young, and Richie Furay and would play seven shows from the planned thirty when, not surprisingly, Young, from Andy Green's piece in *Rolling Stone*, bowed out saying, "I'd be on a tour of my past for the rest of fucking time. I have to be able to move forward. I can't be relegated. I did enough of it for right then." Stills was upset at Young, but soon realized that "when Neil is involved in anything you need a seatbelt." Furay's frustration at his former bandmate's ability to abort the tour also was short-lived, despite the overwhelming success of the seven performances, as, quoted by Jeff Giles, he remarked, "I think everybody was having fun. What was 30 days out of your life . . . But Neil, his idea was, you know,

'I don't want to go back and play those old songs.' So what did he do? He went out and he played all the old songs with Crazy Horse again. But that's his thing."

More recently (2018), as a testament to Buffalo Springfield's enduring popularity, Richie Furay organized a Buffalo Springfield tribute in Los Angeles, inviting Elliot Easton (the Cars), Mickey Dolenz (the Monkees), Iain Mathews (Fairport Convention), Susan Cowsill (Cowsills), Terry Reid, Carla Olson (Textones), Martha Davis (the Motels), the Dream Syndicate, the Three O'Clock, and Gary Myrick.

What Buffalo Springfield might have achieved if they had recorded more than three albums is worth contemplating. To be so admired and influential with so few recordings remains unprecedented in rock annals. Given what Stephen Stills, Neil Young, and Richie Furay accomplished after Buffalo Springfield as solo artists as well as members of Crosby, Stills & Nash, Crosby, Stills, Nash & Young, Manassas (Stills); Crosby, Stills, Nash & Young, Crazy Horse (Young); and Poco, the Souther-Hillman-Furay Band (Furay) begs the question—What if? Members of the group have regretted that a live Buffalo Springfield album was never made. From most accounts, they sounded even better live than in the studio, and those lucky enough to have been at a Springfield performance have verified this statement.

Ben Wener of the *Orange County Register* does not hesitate to rank Buffalo Springfield near the top of his list of Americana's leading pioneers: "Their importance cannot be overstated: The band that the locals used to call the Herd rank only behind Bob Dylan (especially with the Hawks/Band) and the Byrds (with and without Gram Parsons) as the most crucial cornerstones of what's now called Americana music, that hard-to-define yet easy-to-spot hybrid of folk, rock, country, blues, psychedelia and lyrical poetry."

Artists Who Influenced Buffalo Springfield

Bob Dylan, the Beatles, the Everly Brothers, the Rolling Stones, Simon & Garfunkel, the Hollies, Buck Owens, the Byrds, and Tom Paxton.

Americana Artists Influenced by Buffalo Springfield

Beachwood Sparks, Wilco, the Jayhawks, Rosanne Cash, Uncle Tupelo, GospelbeacH, My Morning Jacket, Liquor Giants, and the Asteroid No. 4.

The Grateful Dead

"Jerry Garcia and I were huge into Buck Owens particularly—and Dolly Parton, we were more than smitten."
(Bob Weir)

As noted, Los Angeles provided be a fertile landscape for those artists who helped shape the Americana music genre. But the San Francisco Bay Area also can claim to be of historical significance in melding many musical styles and producing artists who have impacted Americana's evolution: Jefferson Airplane, Moby Grape, Quicksilver Messenger Service, It's a Beautiful Day, the Beau Brummels, New Riders of the Purple Sage, Hot Tuna, Country Joe and the Fish, Creedence Clearwater Revival, Sly and the Family Stone, the Steve Miller Band, and, particularly, the Grateful Dead.

Formed in 1965, the Grateful Dead with original members Jerry Garcia (lead guitar, vocals), Bob Weir (rhythm guitar, vocals), Phil Lesh (bass, vocals), Bill Kreutzman (drums), [Mickey Hart, a second drummer, would join the group in 1967], and Ron "Pigpen" McKernan (keyboards, harmonica vocals) were a psychedelic-rock band whose first three studio albums—*The Grateful Dead* (1967), *Anthem of the Sun* (1968), and *Aoxomoxoa* (1969)— explored an adventurous mixture of folk, jug-band, blues-rock, acid-rock, and experimental-rock styles. Improvisation and lengthy instrumental jams, staples of the Dead's live performances, also were featured on these recordings. These records and the live shows that followed gave birth to an ardent cult of fans famously known as Deadheads, and yet the Grateful Dead still had not captured widespread attention outside the West Coast. This small contingent of concertgoers, however, would explode in scale with the releases of the 1970 back-to-back studio albums, *Workingman's Dead* and *American Beauty*.

A chief characteristic of the born leader, the musical trailblazer, is a willingness to take risks, to follow the heart. Bob Dylan achieved this with *John Wesley Harding* as did the Byrds with *Sweetheart of the Rodeo*, and the Grateful Dead took a gamble that paid enormous dividends both artistically and commercially. Previous to their groundbreaking releases, Dylan and the Byrds had already introduced country and country-rock elements in their songs, so the transformation was not nearly as dramatic as the songwriting shift had to have been for the Dead, whose previous compositions were clearly not roots-based. On a

DVD, drummer Mickey Hart would explain the Dead's radical change in musical format as "stepping out of our spacesuit and coming down to Earth and putting on a pair of Osh Kosh and digging the furrows."

An inspiration, perhaps unconsciously, for the *Workingman's Dead* and *American Beauty* recordings could have been a reaction to the tumultuous ending of the 1960s: when the Summer of Love had lost its shimmer, when violence broke out at the 1968 Democratic National Convention, when Presidential candidate Robert F. Kennedy and Civil Rights Leader Martin Luther King, Jr. were assassinated, when the grisly Manson Family murders shocked America, and when a member of the Hells Angels stabbed a concertgoer to death at the Altamont Speedway Free Festival. The calming, roots-fueled tracks offered a peaceful, soothing respite from the political and social turmoil of the time.

For their genre-blurring travels, and the folk-rock/country-rock layers specifically, in *Workingman's Dead*, Jerry Garcia added the pedal steel guitar and banjo and with longtime songwriting partner, Robert Hunter, composed lyrics that bassist Phil Lesh, from his book, said:

> Reflected an "old, weird" America that perhaps never was . . . The almost miraculous appearance of these new songs would also generate a massive paradigm shift in our group mind: from the mid-munching frenzy of a seven headed fire-breathing dragon to the warmth and serenity of a choir of chanting cherubim. Even the album cover reflects this new direction: the cover of *Aoxomoxoa* is colorful and psychedelic, and that of *Workingman's Dead* is monochromatic and sepia.

Of the eight Grateful Dead originals, Garcia and Hunter combined to write six, while Hunter wrote one and Lesh another with Garcia and Hunter.

Workingman's Dead is classic Americana with the first track on side one, "Uncle John's Band," a prime example. Acoustic rather than electric guitars joined by tight bluegrass harmonies in a folk-rock setting gently sustain the hopeful sentiments of the words. The song has been covered by Jimmy Buffet, Indigo Girls, and Crosby, Stills, & Nash. On track two, "High Time," Garcia's plaintive voice flawlessly fits this country blues tune. "Dire Wolf," track three, displays Garcia's impressive pedal steel talent while track four, "New Speedway Boogie," shows off his vocal range and guitar virtuosity in this electric blues gem. Banjo and Bill Monroe-style high harmonies bolster the bluegrassy "Cumberland Blues," track five, and Delta blues is the genre of choice in the poignantly mournful "Black Peter." "Easy Wind," an electric blues rocker highlighted by "Pigpen" McKernan's harmonica, and the catchy "Casey Jones," one of the Dead's most enduring songs about a railroad engineer who is "high on cocaine," conclude the album.

Chris Willman from *Billboard* magazine had an opportunity to interview the Grateful Dead's Bob during Weir's appearance at the 17th Annual Americana Music Festival & Conference in 2016. Like Gram Parsons, Weir admired country legend Buck Owens:

> Jerry (Garcia) and I were huge into Buck Owens particularly and Dolly Parton, we weren't the only guys listening to Buck Owens. If you listen to the early Beatles records, they were huge into him. I haven't spoken to those guys about it, but I can just hear it in their music. Yeah, they did a Buck Owens tune ["Act Naturally"], but it's more than that. Paul McCartney can play a better

Bakersville shuffle than, I venture to say, anyone in this town [Nashville] today.

Besides the Owens factor in fashioning *Workingman's Dead*, the band's close ties with Crosby, Stills & Nash rubbed off on the Dead and yielded substantially improved harmonies as Jerry Garcia told Jake Woodward: "Hearing those guys sing and how nice they sounded together, we thought, 'We can try that. Let's work on it a little.'" The presence of a pedal steel guitar and banjo in Garcia's hands countrified the sound. Remarkably, Garcia, who had begun to learn how to play a pedal steel a year earlier, would quickly master the instrument and be regularly asked by many artists, including Jefferson Airplane and Crosby, Stills, Nash & Young (collectively and as solo artists), to play the instrument on their recordings. In an article titled "Jerry Garcia and the Pedal Steel Guitar," the author addresses Garcia's style:

> Nashville pedal steel players consider Garcia's playing mediocre. But sometimes technical prowess doesn't make for the best music. Jerry Garcia was an improviser. His playing was intuitive. He was truly one of a kind. He transcended this instrument and made listeners FEEL! He took us to new frontiers, and he still takes us on auditory adventures every time he plucks a note on this instrument he spun into gold.

Speaking of pedal steel guitar players, the years between 1965-1974 produced some of the best ever: Neil Flanz, Rusty Young, "Sneaky" Pete Kleinow, Jaydee Maness, "Red" Rhodes, Al Perkins, and Buddy Emmons. All are connected with several of the Americana trailblazers. Canadian Neil Flanz toured with Gram Parsons and

Emmylou Harris as a member of the Fallen Angels Band. Rusty Young played with Buffalo Springfield and shortly thereafter became a founding member (along with ex-Springfield musicians Jim Messina and Richie Furay) of the influential country-rock band Poco. "Sneaky" Pete Kleinow famously performed with the Flying Burrito Brothers; Jaydee Maness with Gram Parsons and the Byrds. "Red" Rhodes played pedal steel on the Byrds' *Notorious Byrd Brothers* album, and Al Perkins and Buddy Emmons recorded with Gram Parsons. It is no surprise that each of these extraordinary musicians has been inducted into the Steel Guitar Hall of Fame. The emergence of the pedal steel guitar as a featured instrument during these years connected rock and roll to country music and firmly established its popular place among future Americana artists.

Almost as soon as *Workingman's Dead* was released, the Dead returned to the studio and began recording in a style found on the previous album, what today could be labeled Americana. Five of the ten songs again were written by the Garcia/ Hunter team: "Candy Man," "Brokedown Palace," "Till the Morning Comes," and "Attics of My Life." The songwriting credits were spread out compared with *Workingman's Dead*: Garcia/Dawson/Hunter authored "Friend of the Devil," and Garcia/Lesh/Weir/Hunter composed "Truckin'." "Box of Rain," "Sugar Magnolia" and "Operator" were penned by Lesh/Hunter, Weir/Hunter, and McKernan respectively.

Side one opens with Phil Lesh singing lead vocals on "Box of Rain," a country-rock masterpiece featuring emotionally-tinged harmonizing and honey-sweet pedal-steel playing. On track two guest artist Dave Grisman's mandolin evocatively embellishes the lyric and the pleasing acoustic-guitar playing on "Friend of the Devil," like "Box of Rain" one of the most beloved songs in the Grateful Dead canon. The third tune and another Dead classic, "Sugar Magnolia," is a love song favored for its irresistibly appealing refrain and buoyant beat. Songs four and five on side one, "Operator" and "Candyman," exhibit the Grateful Dead's natural grasp of country blues.

"Ripple," a soothing, folk-rock spiritual and a Grateful Dead standard, starts side two. The next tune, "Brokedown Palace," with its gentle, gospel-style intonations, complements "Ripple." Track three on the second side, "Till the Morning Comes," is carried by Byrds-like vocals. "Attics of My Life" follows with perhaps the most exquisite harmonies the Dead ever recorded. And the record ends with the much loved "Truckin'," which, despite its infectious, electric-blues rhythm and drug references, thematically conforms to the acoustically-laden numbers preceding it.

In 1991 (prior to the band's disbandment in 1995) a tribute album, *Deadicated: A Tribute to the Grateful Dead*, was released and drew upon the talents of a celebrated and diverse collection of artists, including Los Lobos, Bruce Hornsby and the Range, Elvis Costello, Suzanne Vega, Dwight Yoakam, Warren Zevon with David Lindley, Indigo Girls, Lyle Lovett, Cowboy Junkies, Dr. John, and Jane's Addiction, evidence of the Dead's influence on artists who work in disparate genres. The two records examined in this chapter, like the tribute LP, reflect the group's genre-blurring style.

That *Workingman's Dead* and *American Beauty* are considered not only the Grateful Dead's best studio efforts but the finest examples of trailblazing Americana masterpieces is not surprising. As Greg Kot, music critic at the *Chicago Tribune* exclaims:

> Despite all those hoary associations with hippies and the free-love generations, the Dead were musical postmodernists in the extreme. The internet helped facilitate cross-cultural blending—not just sampling, but

mixing and remixing styles of music that previously didn't go together. The Dead saw it coming. They stirred up a thick soup of Americana (from blues and bluegrass to jazz, rock and folk) with avant-garde seasoning.

Artists Who Influenced the Grateful Dead

Bob Dylan, Chuck Berry, Buddy Holly, Muddy Waters, Hank Williams, Doc Watson, Crosby, Stills & Nash, the Beatles, Merle Haggard, Buck Owens, Mississippi Sheiks, Woody Guthrie, the Byrds, Ramblin' Jack Elliott, Howlin' Wolf, Rev. Gary Davis, Cannon's Jug Stompers, Elmore James, Charley Patton, Elizabeth Cotten, and Jimmy Reed.

Americana Artists Influenced by the Grateful Dead

Wilco, the Jayhawks, Gov't Mule, Phish, Leftover Salmon, moe., the String Cheese Incident, Cordovas, North Mississippi Allstars, and Blues Traveler.

The Band

> "The rock star stuff never came up for us. The Band was never attacked by groupies before, during or after any show they played."
> (Levon Helm)

Another Canadian-American band (the other being Buffalo Springfield) deserving a place among Americana's trailblazers just might be the first true Americana group. No band found as much inspiration from a wider range of genres—R&B, jump blues, boogie-woogie, swing, jazz, Cajun, country, rockabilly, rock and roll, folk, folk rock, and roots rock—than did the Band. And no rock group boasted as many multi-instrumentalists who were as musically gifted: Rick Danko (vocals, bass, fiddle, guitar); Levon Helm (vocals, drums, tambourine, mandolin, harmonica); Garth Hudson (piano, Lowrey organ, clavinet, alto, tenor, soprano, baritone, and bass saxophones, accordion); Richard Manuel (vocals, keyboards, drums, lap steel guitar); and Robbie Robertson (vocals, guitar). All were first-rate songwriters as well.

Born in Blayney, Ontario, Rick Danko became an early fan of blues, R&B, and country music in his teens, admiring, in particular, Hank Williams and Sam Cooke. Levon Helm, the only American in the group, spent his Arkansan youth admiring Sony Boy Williamson II, the great R&B harmonica player, and especially Sonny Boy's drummer, James "Peck" Curtis. Helm, who would sing lead on most of the Band's songs, couldn't get enough of recording stars Elvis Presley, Conway Twitty, and Bo Diddley, whom he saw perform in person. Garth Hudson as a Windsor, Ontario youth studied and played classical piano before joining the Capers, a rock band, at age 21. Richard Manuel, also from Ontario (Stratford), drew inspiration from R&B legends Ray Charles and Jimmy Reed. Toronto-born Robbie Robertson, like his future bandmates, caught the rock and roll bug early on and would begin playing in bands at age 14.

The Band first got together in Toronto as the Hawks, the backing band for American rockabilly singer Ronnie Hawkins, credited with jumpstarting the rock and roll machine in Canada in the late 1950s and early 1960s. Between 1958 and 1963, the lineup that would evolve into the Band joined Ronnie Hawkins one by one. Drummer Levon Helm, only seventeen at the time, vividly recalled his first show with Hawkins in his autobiography, *This Wheel's on Fire*:

> That first gig was great. Ronnie Hawkins could really work a crowd on Friday night. I

mean he had 'em where he wanted 'em. He was big, good-looking, funny, and had a good voice. He was an entertainer rather than a musician. He had an instinct for crowd psychology and could start a rumble across the room if he wanted by just flicking his wrist. It was this power he had over people. We'd hit that Bo Diddley beat, Hawk would come to the front of the stage and do his kick, that camel walk, and the thing would just take off. Ronnie had been a professional diver as a teenager, so he could execute a front flip into a split that would astonish you. Then he'd dance over and pretend to wind up Will Pop Jones, a big strong kid who hit those piano keys so hard they'd break. God, that rhythm was awesome! I didn't really know what I was doing on the drums, so I just kept time. People danced, so I figured everything was on target. After the show Ronnie gave me fifteen bucks, and I was in heaven.

Recognized soon as Toronto's finest rock ensemble and with their musical craftsmanship under Hawkins continuing to become more polished, in late 1963, the Hawks left their frontman. Lead guitarist Robbie Robertson, as quoted in Back to the Land, said, "Eventually, Hawkins built us up to the point where we outgrew the music and had to leave. He shot himself in the foot, bless his heart, by sharpening us into such a crackerjack band that we had to go out into the world, because we knew what his vision was for himself, and we were all younger and more ambitious musically." Helm, Robertson, Danko, Manuel, and Hudson were ready to play original compositions. They grew weary of repeatedly playing the same songs. Despite the popularity they attained as members of Ronnie Hawkins and the Hawks and the risk of losing steady employment, the born leader/trailblazer gene had kicked in. They were now Levon and the Hawks.

Bob Dylan, who had recently and controversially gone "electric" in 1965, went scouting for a backup band for a U.S. tour. After watching the Hawks in a Toronto club, Dylan was impressed enough to hire them. The concert tour between September 1965 and May 1966 was billed as Bob Dylan and the Band. As discussed earlier, Dylan and the Hawks endured mostly negative (and often hostile) reactions from the press and concertgoers, particularly those who could not forgive Dylan for moving away from his folk roots. An assortment of disruptive behaviors, including incessant heckling, was enough to force Levon Helm, as stated in his book, to leave the tour after only one month: "The whole booing thing became heartbreaking, considering the effort Bob was putting out and how easy it would have been to play it safe. I was starting to get reel pissed off. It was better for me not to be a part of it."

Following the tour and after the release of *Blonde on Blonde*, Bob Dylan was seriously injured in a motorcycle accident near Woodstock, New York. During his long recovery, Dylan and the Hawks reunited in 1967 and began to put down some tracks. These songs, recorded in a pink house that three Hawks (Hudson, Danko, and Manuel) rented in nearby West Saugerties ("Big Pink") and also in Dylan's house, would years later (1975) find their way onto the album *The Basement Tapes*.

Having profited as musicians and songwriters from the Dylan alliance, the Band, as they were now called, scored a record deal with Capitol and in 1968 released *Music from Big Pink*. The album represents a defining moment in the evolution of the Americana ethos. As quoted in Craig Harris's *The Band: Pioneers of Americana Music*, Robbie Robertson explains:

"We liked stuff that had a timeless quality to it. We gathered all these pieces of music and pulled them together, not talking about it. It was a natural procedure and the depth that we were looking for, and the type of storytelling. All these things had an opportunity to be seasoned in a way that, when we were writing and working on music, you could feel that it had years and years of being in a wine keg . . . [*Music from Big Pink*] had nothing to do with what we had done as kids with Ronnie Hawkins and the Hawks, nothing to do with what we did with Dylan. These were precise stories and emotional experiences. Discovering the soul of music was what was important, getting a song across as much emotion as we could—that was the objective, not flailing away, and blasting the walls down. That had nothing to do with it any longer."

Levon Helm, in his autobiography, adds, "The trend at that time was the acid rock phase. That was the new trend, the new fad that was going on, and tune in, turn on, and drop out—hate your mom and dad, don't trust anyone over thirty, and a bunch of other stuff that didn't make a lot of sense. We steered clear of all that and tried to keep it on musical terms."

Mentor, friend, and fellow musician, Bob Dylan, did not play on *Music from Big Pink* but did contribute three songs: "Tears of Rage' (co-written with Richard Manuel), "This Wheel's on Fire" (co-written with Rick Danko), and "I Shall Be Released." He also provided the album cover painting. A Lefty Frizzel cover and seven originals complete the track listings. Of all the tracks the best known is "The Weight," a roots-rock number composed by Robbie

Robertson about a narrator's travels to a town (Nazareth) filled with Biblical allusions and memorable, real-life-inspired characters. Remarkably, the "The Weight," owing to its cross-genre appeal, was covered within one year by R&B and soul icons Jackie DeShannon, Diana Ross & the Supremes and the Temptations, and Aretha Franklin. Underscoring the track's capacity to attract a diverse range of artists are notable renditions from Spooky Tooth, the Staple Singers, Dionne Warwick, the Chambers Brothers, Ringo Starr & His All-Starr Band, John Denver, Weezer, Hoyt Axton, Lee Ann Womack, Joe Cocker, Waylon Jennings & the Waymore Blues Band, and Rickie Lee Jones.

  The somber, slow-paced "Tears of Rage" also has been recorded by a who's who list of artists, including Jimi Hendrix, Gene Clark, Jerry Garcia, Ian & Sylvia, Albert Lee, and Joan Baez. Manuel's intensely emotional vocals drive the aching account of a daughter's rejection of her father (Cordelia/King Lear?) and a theme about the brevity of life. Manuel's "In a Station," as Levon Helm wrote in his autobiography, "is Richard's song about Overlook Mountain and the relative peace we were all feeling after those long years living on the road. He used to laugh and call it his George Harrison song, by which he meant it was spiritual." The cryptic, Dylanesque lyrics of Danko's "Caledonia Mission," as with many of the songs from *Big Pink*, offer multiple interpretations. A song's meaning is not easily, if ever, detected. But it is the music behind the lyrics which resonates more powerfully in an album that Stephen Thomas Erlewine, from *Pitchfork* magazine, calls "revolutionary." The ambiguous tenets of what would later be called "Americana" appear more clearly after reading Erlewine's musings:

> The striking thing about the Band's debut album is how its story hasn't changed since its release in the summer of 1968, when it

> provided a tonic to the overblown psychedelia swamping the late 1960s . . . At the time, George Harrison and Eric Clapton cited the album as the reason why they decided to abandon overdriven blues and psychedelia to pursue a path of quiet contemplation and authenticity . . . From the outset, its originality was described in terms of genre, how *Music from Big Pink* draws from a number of American roots music—country, blues, gospel, folk, gospel, rockabilly—without ever sounding distinctly like one of its inspirations . . . The way it makes roots music sound as impressionistic and idiosyncratic as any other kind of rock 'n' roll is revolutionary.

Worth noting are the humorous and ingeniously constructed "We Can Talk," which features Helm, Manuel, and Danko exchanging the lead vocals to replicate a conversation between the three; Garth Hudson's towering Lowrey Organ intro on "Chest Fever"; a gospel-blues cover of Dylan's "I Shall Be Released"; and a stirring country rocker with the Band's distinctive vocals and musicianship, "This Wheel's on Fire," a song later covered by the Byrds, Phil Lesh, Elvis Costello, the Hollies, and Ian and Sylvia, among others.

The reviews, then and now, have been uniformly stellar. Tom Power from *CBC Music* claims that "*Music from Big Pink* has been a major influence on any roots band worth its salt. Without it you wouldn't have Wilco, Ryan Adams, Patty Loveless, or Mumford & Sons." *Rolling Stone* magazine ranked it at #34 among its list of the 500 greatest albums of all time, and Roger Waters, exuberant in his praise, told Prog Archives: "That one record changed everything for me. After *Sgt. Pepper* it's the most influential record in the history of rock and roll. It affected Pink Floyd deeply, deeply, deeply. Philosophically, other albums may have been more important, like Lennon's first solo album. But sonically, I think *Music from Big Pink* is fundamental to everything that happened after it."

The next studio release, *The Band* (1969), once again displayed the musical virtuosity and originality found on *Music from Big Pink* but offered more songs written or co-written by Robbie Robertson (all 12, in fact) and more tracks with characters and places related to America's past. The Band's pioneering roots-rock sound perfectly complemented a bygone era that the group vividly attempted to capture. Side one opens with "Across the Great Divide," an upbeat, amusing tale which surprisingly begins, ironically, with a wife ("Molly") pointing a gun at her husband. The lyrics and instrumentation combine to create a scene right out of an Old Western movie or the American South. Next, a hillbilly who has trouble controlling his girlfriend is the subject of the ragtime number, "Rag Mama Rag." One of the Band's most admired songs, "The Night They Drove Old Dixie Down," the third cut on side one, sympathetically describes the plight of a poor, white Virginian ("Virgil Cane") near the end of the Civil War. The song has been recorded by Joan Baez, Johnny Cash, the Allman Brothers Band, Richie Havens, the Black Crowes, and the Jerry Garcia Band, just to mention a handful. Track number five on the first side, "Up on Cripple Creek," oozes funk by means of Garth Hudson playing the clavinet with a wah-wah pedal, and has as its narrator a truck driver who describes his fun antics (gambling, drinking, etc.) in Louisiana with a woman named "Bessie," who is not his wife.

Laced with double entendres and testosterone-driven rhythms, side two opens with "Jemima Surrender," described by Helm in his book as a song "about wanting the love of a lady of color." Track three, another rocker, "Look Out Cleveland," describes the confusion and panic in

Cleveland, Texas as an approaching storm appears imminent. Songmango.com pays respect to the musical dexterity and imagery of the Band on this number:

> As the heavy weather approaches—whether it is apocalyptic or only a royal pain in the ass—the music intensifies just as a storm would. One of the great skills the Band has is to take the mundane, inflate it to the archetypal, then delete it in order to bring it back down to earth again. Additionally, there is some aw-shucks humor in their songs, a slight tongue-in-cheek attitude that is like a swirl of decorative icing on a homemade red velvet cake. . . The Band's songs are populated with characters. In this case, Ben Pike; the justice of the peace; and, later on, the nursery rhyme's old woman who lived in a shoe pop on and off stage.

The last two songs on side two, once again set in the South during an earlier time in American history, illustrate the plight of the simple, often forsaken individual. "The Unfaithful Servant," a jazz-inspired track set in the South, gives a sympathetic rendering of a servant who is released from his job, and "King Harvest (Has Surely Come)," a compassionate narrative about a skid-row farmer.

Rolling Stone columnist Ralph J. Gleason in his 1969 review expressed wonder at the album's capacity to generate images of an older America:

> I hear these songs as a sound track to James Agee's *Let Us Now Praise Famous Men,* to the real documentary of the American truth. They are sparse songs with never a superfluous note or unnecessary syllable.

> And yet the sparseness, like a Picasso line, is so right that it implies everything needed. Lean and dusty, perhaps, like Henry Fonda walking down the road at the beginning of *Grapes of Wrath*, it says volumes in a phrase. . . They could have called the album America, Robbie says, and after you play it a few times you know what he means. We live in these cities and we forget that there is more than 3000 miles between New York and the smog of Los Angeles and those 3000 miles are deeply rooted to another world in another time and with another set of values.

Mary Chapin Carpenter, from an article titled "This Music Made Me: Mary Chapin Carpenter," summed up her feeling for *The Band*: "Every song on this album kills me. The Band were incredibly important to me as I was growing up. They had such a handmade quality to what they did, but it was never precious or frail, just utterly original."

The next studio album from the Band, *Stage Fright* (1970), may not have been as universally well-received by music critics as the first two LPs, and yet it actually outdid the others on *Billboard*, peaking at number 5. Over time, however, reviews have turned more favorable (a recurring theme with a handful of albums from Americana's trailblazers.) Also, as noted earlier, the trailblazing artist, the born leader, will take risks and follow an uncharted musical path. It was no different with the Band's third release. *Stage Fright* offered a more personal, less historical aesthetic. It also delivered more rock than roots as reviewer Nick DeRiso points out: "The Band simply tears through them [the songs]. A return to the road that chiseled their sound. They attacked *Stage Fright* with a muscularity unheard since their days backing Bob Dylan and Ronnie Hawkins." This new direction extended to the production with the presence of

Todd Rundgren as engineer and the Band as producers for the first time. The one constant was Robbie Robertson as the group's chief songwriter and co-writer, owning full or partial song credits for all ten tracks.

Stage Fright was darker, more confessional than either *Big Pink* or *The Band*. Personal issues began to erode the band's camaraderie as Levon Helm recalled in *This Wheel's on Fire*:

> *Stage Fright* was when everything changed for us. It was an immense turning point, something that was obvious to anyone who bought the record. . . Rick Danko: "If you've never made a million dollars overnight like we did, you have no concept of what it can do. We saw it ruin people—kill them! Suddenly we had all the money we needed, and people were falling over themselves to make us happy, which meant giving us all the dope we could stand." . . . Heroin was around Woodstock, around New York [where the album was recorded]. It was everywhere. Being a musician, you couldn't avoid it. . . Robbie Robertson has referred to the *Stage Fright* era as "The Darkness," by which he means this period of addiction and dissolution. But I remember that the drugs were just part of the black mood that settled upon us. There were also issues of artistic control of the Band and the direction we were going in—if any.

Side one opens with "Strawberry Wine," a bluesy rocker reminiscent of "Jemima Surrender"; track two, "Sleeping," a song about the respite sleep provides from life troubles, jumps from a torpid tempo to a brisk jazz beat and back again; track three, the joyful, upbeat "Time to Kill," is one of the most catchy songs in the Band's body of work; track four, the rollicking "Just Another Whistle Stop," submits a personal account of the travails that await us on the train called life; the fifth and final track on side one, the prayerful "All La Glory," tenderly expresses how Levon Helm's vocals work equally well on a lullaby as they do on a rocker. Robertson's guitar and Hudson's Wurlitzer sweeten the effect.

"The Shape I'm in," the funky, autobiographical first track on side two and one of the Band's most popular songs, showcases Manuel's vocals and, through the lyrics, a stressful time in the lives of the bandmates; track two, "The W.S. Walcott Medicine Show," as Craig Harris writes, was connected to Levon Helm's childhood memories in Arkansas:

> As a youngster, he loved the performances of the African American medicine and minstrel shows, including F.S. Walcott's Rabbit's Foot Minstrels, who traveled the South from 1900 to 1960, bringing top-notch black entertainers, Ma Rainey, Bessie Smith, Big Joe Williams, Brownie McGhee, Rufus Thomas and Louis Jordan to audiences of all races. Helm's memories had inspired the Robertson-penned "The W.S. Walcott Medicine Show" and "Life Is a Carnival."

Track four, the allegorical and Appalachian-tinged "Daniel and the Sacred Harp," reflects the group's personal struggles at this time through the theme of selling one's soul for music. Side two's final track, the bittersweet "The Rumor," highlighted by Helm, Danko, and Manuel trading lead vocals, structurally and lyrically suggests that a healing reconciliation among band members is possible. History would prove otherwise. The Band had reached its zenith.

From Nick DeRiso, these concluding thoughts:

> *Stage Fright* is the story of a group that couldn't be saved from expectation, even when it tried to keep things simple; couldn't be saved from themselves, even as the doomed Richard Manuel [who committed suicide in 1986] slipped inexorably away as a creative force . . . Everything that had happened, all the ways that these men had been irretrievably changed, seemed to have leaked into these songs, one by one. *Stage Fright* may not be as well-regarded as the Band's initial two studio efforts, but it's certainly the bravest of them all. This album didn't fetishize the past, didn't so often seek to cloak things in the parables of age-old wisdom, so much as explore a present that maybe still seems unbelievable today.

The Band, and Buffalo Springfield before them, were dominated by individuals not born in the United States, Canadians specifically. Today, more and more Americana artists hail from countries oceans away. The Americana Music Association UK (AMA-UK), officially formed in London in 2012, has established the same aims as its Nashville counterpart and, likewise, an annual conference, festival and awards ceremony. One of the most popular Americana bands, in fact, is British—Mumford & Sons, who in 2018 won the Trailblazer Award at the UK Americana Awards. As quoted by Alex Gallacher, the band expressed that they were "very honoured to be included in this UK Americana Awards. From 'Folk-Rock' to

'Bluegrass' to 'Country' to 'Folk and Roll' we've never fully felt comfortable with labels that people have put on our music." Their next comments continue to offer a wonderfully compact illustration of the Americana artist: "To us, it's just the sound that we make, drawing on all sorts of influences from America and elsewhere. America encapsulates this patchwork of influence most broadly and to be recognized alongside some of our heroes is truly humbling."

Commenting on the strengthening ties between AMA-US and AMA-UK, Jed Hilly offered an optimistic view about the growth of Americana to interviewer Paul Sexton: "The impact of the relationship between the U.S. and the U.K. is another iteration, and I think Americana is today what the British Invasion was in the '60s. I'm completely inspired to see the Americana community expand around the world.

In 2017 the First Annual Australian Americana Music Honours took place in Melbourne to recognize Country/Americana singer Kasey Chambers and promoter Brian "BT" Taranto. Americana Music Association's Executive Director Jed Hilly hosted the event with Americana favorites Old Crow Medicine Show and Valerie June headlining the list of performers. The 2018 ceremony honored roots-music editor Brian Wise and folk-rocker Shane Howard with live performances from Country/Americana artists Margo Price and Joshua Hedley. (To clarify, the vast majority of artists on the London/Melbourne stages were British and Australian.)

The growing international appeal of Americana music is reflected in Last.fm's list of the top Americana artists:

From Canada: Cowboy Junkies, Neil Young & Crazy Horse, Fred Eaglesmith, Kathleen Edward, Redbird, Romi Mayes, the Duhks, the Deep Dark Woods, Po' Girl, Devon Sproule, Great Lake Swimmers, the Be Good

Tanyas, the Wailin' Jennings, Julie Dorion, Carolyn Mark. <u>From the UK</u>: Billy Bragg, Richard Thompson, the Broken Family Band, King Charles, Beth Orton, Hey Negrita, Noah and the Whale. <u>From Sweden</u>: Invictus, Andre Wall, Norman Wall, First Aid Kit, the Talles Man on Earth, Christian Kjellvander. <u>From Germany</u>: Markus Rill, Digger Barnes. <u>From Norway</u>: Zahl, Jonas Alaska. <u>From Spain</u>: Stormy Mondays. <u>From Belgium</u>: Douglas Firs. <u>From the Netherlands</u>: Ad Vandervan. <u>From New Zealand</u>: the Broadsides.

<u>Artists Who Influenced the Band</u>

Bob Dylan, the Everly Brothers, Carl Perkins, Chuck Berry, the Byrds, Buffalo Springfield, Booker T. & the MG's, Fats Domino, Ronnie Hawkins, Muddy Waters, Duane Eddy, Left Frizzel, Sonny Boy Williamson II, LaVern Baker, Sam Cooke, and Bo Diddley.

<u>Americana Artists Influenced by the Band</u>

The Jayhawks, Mary Chapin Carpenter, Wilco, Uncle Tupelo, Jason & the Scorchers, the Blasters, Golden Smog, the Gourds, Whiskeytown, Last Train Home, Son Volt, Crazy Horse, Wool on Wolves, Shinyribs, and Brinsley Schwarz.

Arlo Guthrie

"I'm not just a singer-songwriter doing
songs in the key of me."
(Arlo Guthrie)

Singer-songwriter, protest, folk, and folk-rock singer, Arlo Guthrie, despite his relative obscurity when compared with the other eight trailblazers, is undoubtedly an influential Americana pioneer. Between 1965 and 1974 Guthrie's musical sensibilities proved to be a closer match to current Americana artists than those from his more acclaimed contemporaries. An original and masterful storyteller, not only did Guthrie incorporate a wider range of musical styles, he also composed lyrics that often spoke more precisely and powerfully to American themes.

    To have as a father the most influential American folksinger, Woody Guthrie, composer of hundreds of folk, political, and children's songs, and yet not be eclipsed by his dad's legacy is a testimony to the son's musical gifts. Arlo Guthrie inherited Woody's songwriting and storytelling skills along with the gene that a singer be obliged to speak out against social injustice. A notable difference between father and son, however, involves instrumentation. Woody Guthrie played guitar, harmonica, mandolin, and fiddle while son Arlo, astonishingly, played acoustic guitar, mandolin, piano, harmonica, banjo, saxophone, clarinet, flute, piccolo, and violin. Add also cowbell, celesta, autoharp, harp, recorder, cor anglais, whistle, and tambourine to the list.

    Arlo Guthrie is best known for his 1967 counterculture, talking-blues, anti-war hit, "Alice's Restaurant Massacree," a satirical, autobiographical narrative of how a citation for littering ironically led to the Vietnam-era U.S. Army's refusal to draft him. At the song's end, listeners are encouraged to sing along to hasten the end of the war. The song inspired the 1969 film *Alice's Restaurant*. Despite its 18-minutes-and-34-seconds length, the song became widely popular, especially with the anti-establishment crowd.

    The Americana components of "Alice's Restaurant Massacree" include the genre (talking blues), invented, according to Steve Legget from AllMusic, in 1926 by Christopher Allen in Bouchillon, a country and blues musician from South Carolina. Woody Guthrie ("Talking Dust Bowl Blues"), Phil Ochs ("Talking Cuban Crisis"), and Bob Dylan ("Talking World War III Blues") occasionally employed this musical form where rhythmic speech supplants singing. Two other Americana elements are Arlo Guthrie's boundary-pushing, groundbreaking, anti-mainstream, and financially-precarious decision to release a song that both lampooned the politically controversial Vietnam War draft and also lasted beyond 18 minutes. The results turned out quite favorable for Guthrie as pointed out in this reflection he made later in his career: "If you do anything for 40 years, you can do it comfortably. And it will always be good. But unless you're willing to risk it being bad, it can never be great."

Arlo Guthrie's first studio album of all originals was *Alice's Restaurant* (1967) with the song "Alice's Restaurant Massacree" taking up the entire first side. Side two displays the folk artist's genre-blurring immediately with "Chilling of the Evening," its psychedelic, folk-rock textures reminiscent of the Byrds and Donovan. Next is a jug band number, "Ring-Around-a-Rosy Rag," followed by the pop-sounding "Now and Then." The fourth cut, "I'm Going Home," is a gently-phrased ballad that leads into the amusing, bluesy "The Motorcycle Song." The Dylanesque "Highway in the Wind," a love song that completes side two, features some of Guthrie's best acoustic guitar work and some of his most heartfelt lyrics.

Briefly mentioned earlier is the musical style called "jug band music," whose origins are rooted among the African-American population in early 1900s, largely in the South. At that time bands employed homemade instruments made from washboards, spoons, stovepipes, gourds, and jugs to replicate the sound of string and brass instruments. (The term "skiffle" is often used in place of jug band.) Arlo

Guthrie and fellow Americana trailblazers like the Grateful Dead were influenced by this style, as were other Americana-related artists, including the Lovin' Spoonful, Country Joe and the Fish, the Youngbloods, Creedence Clearwater Revival, and the Nitty Gritty Dirt Band.

For his 1970 album, *Washington County*, Arlo Guthrie procured the services of a stellar group of musicians, including Hoyt Axton (bass, vocals), Ry Cooder (bottleneck guitar), Doug Dillard (banjo), Chris Ethridge (bass), and Clarence White (electric guitar). Except for Woody Guthrie's "Lay Down Little Doggies" and Bob Dylan's "Percy's Song," eight of the ten tracks were original compositions. Several of the finer songs include "Washington County," a foot-stomping bluegrass instrumental, highlighting Dillard's banjo virtuosity; "Valley to Pray," a gospel tune covered by many artists; and "Percy's Song," a 1963 Dylan ballad about a fatal car crash that Fairport Convention had also covered a year earlier on *Unhalfbricking* (1969).

For his next studio LP, *Hobo's Lullaby* (1972), Arlo Guthrie added musical luminaries Linda Ronstadt (vocals), Spooner Oldham (keyboards), Jim Keltner (drums), and Byron Berline (mandolin, fiddle) to the talented personnel from *Washington County*. On *Hobo's Lullaby*, Americana pioneer Guthrie also invited the following jazz notables to assist: Max Bennet (bass), Cozy Cole (drums), and Wilton Felder (tenor saxophone). Even a professional jug player, Fritz Richmond (washtub bass), was recruited. Surprisingly, only two originals appear among the eleven tracks: "Mapleview (20%) Rag" and "Days Are Short."

The album's most famous track is a cover of Steve Goodman's "City of New Orleans" that became Arlo Guthrie's only Top 40 hit, reaching #4 on the *Billboard* Easy Listening chart. Willie Nelson, John Denver, the Seldom Scene, and Judy Collins also recorded their own versions. The lyrics narrate the end of the life of an actual Illinois

Central Railroad train named The City of New Orleans. Songs about trains is an archetypal topic of folk, country, country-rock, rock, bluegrass, gospel, blues, R&B, and Americana, as in the following examples: "Casey Jones" (the Grateful Dead), "Folsom Prison Blues" (Johnny Cash), "Homeward Bound" (Simon and Garfunkel), "Midnight Train to Georgia" (Gladys Night and the Pips), "Slow Train Coming" (Bob Dylan), and "Wabash Cannonball" (Carter Family).

Smoothly blending a variety of musical styles, Arlo Guthrie covers Hoyt Axton's "Lightning Bar Blues" with his tasty slide guitar licks, Woody Guthrie's classic protest ballad "1913 Massacre," Bob Dylan's pensive "When the Ship Comes In," and Goebel Leon Reeves's folk masterpiece, the gentle, wistful "Hobo's Lullaby," which was also recorded by Arlo Guthrie's father.

Arlo Guthrie is a master at establishing a gentle intimacy with his listeners on recordings (and in live performances especially), as all the tracks on *Hobo's Lullaby* confirm. The smaller venues where Guthrie chooses to perform offer the perfect environment for the deeply personal relationship he develops with his concertgoers—a common goal of Americana artists. Naturally engaging, Guthrie's nimble wit and folksy commentary between songs (and often inside the music as well) famously seal this bond.

Last of the Brooklyn Cowboys (1973) quickly followed *Hobo's* release, and once more Arlo Guthrie surrounded himself with a bevy of gifted musicians, a staggering forty-three. Some of the notable newcomers to a Guthrie studio session included Irish fiddler Kevin Burke, R&B bassist Chuck Rainey, former Byrds and Flying Burrito drummer Gene Parsons, trombonist Dick Hyde, and pedal steel guitarist Jerry Brightman from Buck Owens and the Buckaroos. A musical polymath, Arlo Guthrie invited musicians whose talents represented an astounding amalgamation of styles: classical, rock, southern rock, swamp rock, hard rock, pop, folk, jazz, cool jazz, swing, big band, bebop, soul, funk, R&B, blues, gospel, country, honky-tonk, and country rock. Pedal steel guitar, harpsichord, tabla, accordion, trombone, horn, clarinet, woodwind, oboe, and flute were the instruments added from the previous album.

As expected folk and folk-rock sounds permeate the recording, and the mix of styles beautifully augments the traditional musical elements, creating a fuller, more original effect. Arlo Guthrie honors his father by singing the harmonica, pedal-steel fused "Ramblin' Round" and the Caribbean-flavored "Gypsy Davy." He pays respect to Hank Williams with a yodeling cover of "Lovesick Blues." Guthrie's affection and respect for folk and country pioneers continues with a jazz crooner's phrasing of a Jimmie Rodgers hit "Miss the Mississippi" and a fiddle-charged version of Ernest Tubb's "This Trouble Mind of Mine." And Bob Dylan's surreal folk song "Gates of Eden" is given full band accompaniment. Arlo Guthrie's roots-music binge extends to self-penned products: "Cooper's Lament," a chorused-back R&B track; "Cowboy Song," a winsome country-rocker; "Last Train," a sweet, tender bluegrass gospel; "Uncle Jeff," a Nitty Gritty Dirt Band-sounding ditty; and "Week on the Rag," a ragtime gem.

The final Americana pathfinder album from Arlo Guthrie, *Arlo Guthrie* (1974), consists of seven originals from the eleven tracks. Woody Guthrie's protest ballad "Deportees" and one of his father's popular children's songs, "Bling Blang," along with Jimmy Rodgers' country-western classic "When the Cactus Is in Bloom" and the African-American spiritual "Go Down Moses," are the covers. As was the case with his recent LPs, Guthrie enlisted a flock of prized session musicians, the majority of whom had played with him before. Two guest musicians of note, Buddy Emmons (pedal steel guitar) and the Southern

California Community Choir (choir/chorus) appear for the first time with Guthrie.

Among the originals are a protest song directed against President Nixon, "Presidential Rag"; a country rocker bathed in Buddy Edmonds' animated pedal steel, "Won't Be Long"; a groove-laden R&B track, "Children of Abraham"; a Randy Newman-style rag, "Nostalgia Rag"; a funny, fanciful, children's ballad, "Me and My Goose"; a high-harmony, Bill Monroe-inspired bluegrass number, "Hard Times"; and a gorgeously composed, poignant ballad, "Last to Leave."

Patrick A. Reed, writing in *Depth of Field* magazine, discusses the impact of Arlo Guthrie's musical ethos:

> By 1970, Arlo had credit to burn, was signed to Warner Brothers Records and had some of America's finest musical talent at his disposal. What followed was a sequence of albums that brilliantly blurred genre and style, spawned a major hit ("City of New Orleans"), and blended traditional folk, country, western swing, bluegrass, and a half-dozen other genres into a distinct and individual style of Americana... Arlo honed a sound on these records that was wide-ranging and fiercely unique: a song about a miners strike sits next to a joyous take on "Ukulele Lady," slide guitar blues back up to Irish reel, children's songs and scathing political satire and tender ballads sit side-by-side.

The above passage beautifully expresses Arlo Guthrie's contributions to Americana while offering a clearer understanding of the genre. Reed, however, goes a step further and shares how Guthrie's music impacted him:

And thinking about it, I realize how deeply that very sense of exploration and inclusion affected me, opening my mind and ears to sounds that I can spend the rest of my life learning about, creating a picture that's all the more exciting for its diversity. From cowboy yodeling to barroom storytelling to Appalachian mountain music to songs about trains and farming and corruption and traveling and gypsies and hobos, it's the sound of America and all that it encompasses.

Artists Who Influenced Arlo Guthrie

Woody Guthrie, Bob Dylan, Pete Seeger, the Weavers, Hank Williams, Jimmie Rodgers, Johnny Cash, the Carter Family, Burl Ives, Cisco Houston, and Jean Ritchie.

Americana Artists Influenced By Arlo Guthrie

Mary Chapin Carpenter, John Gorka, Patty Griffin, Richard Buckner, Dar Williams, and Ani DiFranco.

John Prine

"Writing is about a blank piece of paper and leaving out what's not supposed to be there."
(John Prine)

Arguably Americana's preeminent artist, if not its most archetypal, influential singer-songwriter, vocalist and guitarist John Prine wears many hats as a beloved folk, folk-rock, country, country-rock, progressive bluegrass, and Americana artist—and he wears them equally well. No one less than Bob Dylan told Bill Flanagan of *Huffington Post* that John Prine was one of his favorite songwriters: "Prine's stuff is pure Proustian existentialism. Midwestern mindtrips to the nth degree. And he writes beautiful songs." Johnny Cash placed Prine alongside Rodney Crowell, Guy Clark, and Steve Goodman as his four favorite writers. And Roger Waters, far removed stylistically from Prine, was quoted in *Word* magazine as saying that Prine produces "extraordinarily eloquent music—and he lives on that plane with Neil Young and John Lennon."

Mailman, Army soldier, then Chicago-based folk singer, John Prine's career took off in the early 1970s when Kris Kristofferson publicly expressed his respect and delight after seeing Prine perform. At the time Prine was becoming a fixture in the Chicago folk revival movement along with friend and fellow singer-songwriter Steve Goodman. Acclaimed *Chicago Sun-Times* movie critic Roger Ebert actually wrote Prine's first review. Here is an excerpt from Ebert's column on Friday, October 9, 1970: "He appears on stage with such modesty he almost seems to be backing into the spotlight. He sings rather quietly, and his guitar work is good, but he doesn't show off. He starts slow. But after a song or two, even the drunks in the room began to listen to his lyrics. And then he has you."

Roger Ebert was transfixed by songs that would shortly appear on John Prine's debut album, *John Prine* (1971). Immediately lauded by critics upon its release, the album would quickly awaken a strong fan base while introducing some of Prine's most cherished compositions, including "Illegal Smile," "Sam Stone," "Paradise," "Hello in There," "Angel from Montgomery," and "Your Flag Decal Won't Get You Into Heaven," all sung in Prine's inimitable, folksy, wry, bemused, humorous, wistful, topical, and reflective style.

Although Prine has stated that "Illegal Smile" is not about smoking dope, most listeners find it impossible to believe that it isn't given the unambiguous lyrics and the fact that the song was written when marijuana possession was more seriously criminalized. Regardless of whether the song is about "lighting up" or not, all can agree that Prine's humorous spin provides a clearer perspective on a controversial social issue. The poignant "Sam Stone" addresses a grimmer topic, heroin addiction, as the story of a returning Vietnam veteran and his death by overdose reveal. How a coal company scarred the once-pristine Western Kentucky hills is the subject of what has become a bluegrass standard, "Paradise," and has been covered by John Fogerty, Dwight Yoakam, John Denver, the Everly Brothers, Johnny Cash, the Seldom Scene, and Jackie DeShannon. "Angel from Montgomery," about a middle-aged woman's struggle with growing older, is John Prine's most-covered composition. Tanya Tucker, John Denver, Carly Simon, Bonnie Rait, Susan Tedeschi, Old Crow Medicine, Dave Mathews Band and Ben Harper are some of the well-known artists who have recorded the song. "Hello in There" is a heartrending reflection about a lonely old couple. The anti-war folk song "Your Flag Decal Won't Get You into Heaven" wryly assails hollow patriotism.

John Prine includes three more memorable songs: "Spanish Pipedream," a story about a soldier and a topless dancer who encourages him to live simply; "Donald and Lydia," a ballad of two young lovers suffering from loneliness; "Six O'Clock News," an account of a young boy's suicide; and "Quiet Man," a tale about the narrator's epiphany. As with the other cuts all are performed in the genre-blending, Americana style.

An early review (1971) by Karen Berg of *Rolling Stone* magazine foretold the bright future ahead for John Prine:

> This is a very good first album by a very good songwriter. Good songwriters are on the rise, but John Prine is differently good. His work demands some time and thought from the listener—he's not out to write pleasant tunes,

> he wants to arrest the cursory listener and get attention for some important things he has to say and, thankfully, he says them without falling into the common trap of writing with overtones of self-importance or smugness . . . he's a good songwriter but there are indications he can be a great one. In his liner notes Kris Kristofferson writes of Prine: "Twenty-four years old and writes like he's two-hundred and twenty." . . . It's good to have a fine new talent around who is both interesting and provocative. If he's this good this young, time should be on his side.

Berg's observations are validated when Michael H. Little, writing for *Vinyl District* many years later (2013), calls *John Prine*

> The best of his LPs . . . and when push comes to shove all of Prine's LPs are great. But I ain't shitting you when I say that *John Prine* contains at least six bona fide classics, which makes for a ratio of brilliance you'd have to look back to Dylan at his mid-sixties prime to equal, and even its two weakest links are songs that almost any songwriter would be proud to call his own.

Not as well received by critics, John Prine's sophomore release, the bluegrass-imbued (noticeably more dobro, mandolin, and fiddle), *Diamonds in the Rough* (1972), nonetheless pioneered the Americana style while once again composing lyrics and storylines that could only be created inside the fertile and uniquely pliable mind of John Prine: an amusing conversation with a talkative Jesus ("Everybody"); a cheating woman as a metaphor for the Vietnam War ("The

Great Compromise"); a unfaithful wife who runs off with a Fuller Brush salesman ("The Frying Pan"); and a Hank Williams parody with a perfect title ('Yes I Guess They Oughta Name a Drink After You").

Diamonds, recorded in only three days, did include a John Prine standard, "Souvenirs," a bittersweet ballad often performed with his close friend and fellow songwriter Steve Goodman, whose most famous composition was "City of New Orleans." The song would later appear on *Souvenirs* (2000) a studio album of fresh recordings of earlier Prine favorites with "Sam Stone," "Angel from Montgomery," "Hello in There," and "Donald and Lydia" as a few examples.

An article which reviews John Prine's 1975 album, *Common Sense*, gives high marks to *Diamonds in the Rough*:

> Prine's second album, *Diamonds in the Rough*, was panned when it came out, but in many ways it is an improvement over the first. While there is nothing that can match the perfection of "Paradise" or the pathos of "Angel from Montgomery," the best thing about the album is that Prine starts to loosen up a little, and loosening up is a key that opens the door to the entire rest of what has proven to be a spectacular career. . . If the first album took itself a little too seriously, *Diamonds in the Rough* has the feel of something intended to be a minor effort, which isn't a knock on the album; in fact, that is precisely what makes it a step forward from *John Prine*. What is becoming evident with this material is that the more Prine allows himself to have a sense of humor, the better his work will be.

Before looking at a third Prine record made between 1965 and 1974, the years established in this book as those when the Americana trailblazers emerged, a born leader/pathfinder trait mentioned before is how initially these artists' releases sometimes were met with poor reviews and even poorer sales but how later these same recordings became recognized as jewels: the Byrds' *Sweetheart of the Rodeo* was a commercial flop; none of Gram Parsons' or Gene Clark's groundbreaking albums made as much as a small dent on the *Billboard* chart; and *Diamonds in the Rough* produced as many negative as it did positive reviews.

One explanation as to why an Americana trailblazer's work was ignored, lukewarmly received, or skewered by listeners or critics is that the musical risks taken, as with *Sweetheart of the Rodeo*, for instance, dramatically upset audience expectations. The seismic shift in musical direction came too suddenly. The open-minded listener and those who played the record a few more times before rushing to judgment, however, were rewarded with an exceptional and enduring experience.

In general, the Americana trailblazers stand apart from their contemporaries by either ignoring or not caring about the consequences of pursuing an original musical vision. Over time their efforts are usually appreciated. More popular now than when he lived, Gram Parsons, for example, did not attain legendary status until many years after his death in 1973. John Prine's stature, conversely, started strong and has gained momentum to this day. Prine's third album, *Sweet Revenge* (1974), had a lot to do with that.

Unlike the first two albums, John Prine was backed by a considerably larger group of session musicians, which added a fuller sound (especially when compared with *Diamonds*) behind his improved vocals and potent songwriting. Only one song among the twelve tracks, the traditional "Nine Pound Hammer," was not composed by Prine. *Sweet Revenge* is the recording that, as Tom Nolan wrote in his review, offers "another side of John Prine, a departure from the unrelenting somberness of his earlier work, and an engaging picture of the social being beneath the social conscience." Nolan goes on to say that "it's a more human work, more mature, and a step forward artistically and toward a wider audience." To paraphrase Nolan's remarks, John Prine discovered his true voice on *Sweet Revenge*, a voice that remained on the many recordings that followed.

Prine's idiosyncratic and brilliant songwriting unites all the songs, from the absurdly funny "Please Don't Bury Me" to a loving yet unsentimental, wistful country-folk tribute to his grandfather, "Grandpa Was a Carpenter." The imagery in the touching ballad "Christmas in Prison" is striking in its capacity to both mesmerize and be deeply felt. "Sweet Revenge" is Prine's outlaw-country answer to those critics who wrote negative reviews of his second album. A Spanish-guitar interlude intensifies the reflective nature of "A Good Time," and the rollicking "Mexican Home" once more reveals the lyrical artistry that decorates *Sweet Revenge* and distinguishes John Prine from most songwriters.

Juli Thanki, in a 2017 article titled "John Prine: The Godfather of Americana Music," states how, "forty-six years after release of his masterful, eponymous debut album, the mailman-turned-songwriter, whose empathy and off-kilter sense of humor has been at the root of music spanning almost half a century, is hotter than ever." Prine has won over a dozen music awards in a wide range of categories from a diverse group of organizations: the Association for Independent Music (AFIM), the Grammy Awards, the American Music Honors & Awards, the Nashville Songwriters Hall of Fame, the UK's BBC Radio 2, the PEN/Song Lyrics Award, and the International Bluegrass Music Awards. Those include the AFIM Indie Award for Folk Music (1991) for *The Missing Years*; the AFIM Indie

Award for Rock Music for *Lost Dogs and Mixed Blessings* (1995); three Grammys for Best Contemporary Folk Album (1992 and 2006) for *The Missing Years* and *Fair & Square* and the Hall of Fame Award; four Americana Music Awards—the Lifetime Achievement Award of Songwriting (2003) and Artist of the Year (2005, 2017, 2018); the Hall of Fame Induction Award (2003) from the Nashville Songwriters HOF; another Lifetime Achievement Award (2003) from BBC Radio 2; and the PEN Song Lyrics Award (2016).

If Emmylou Harris is the Queen of Americana, then John Prine must be its King. John Prine is the most Americana of any Americana artist as Rick Bass proves with these perceptive observations:

> John Prine has been writing songs and making records—20 of them—since 1971. He's never had a true hit single or upended the Nashville music machine, the way Waylon, Willie, and the rest of the Outlaws did... Nonetheless, Prine is among the most revered and influential country artists of all time, having gained a notoriety not for his antics or charisma but for his ability to turn a phrase ... he has amassed a legion of fans, who cherish him like the world's greatest secret. Kris Kristofferson, who discovered him, once said Prine was so good that other musicians were "going to have to break his fingers." . . . Prine is often compared to Dylan. But while Dylan is a poet, Prine is a storyteller... He is a sucker for a good punch line, and on stage, he laughs at his own jokes the way your grandfather might. To say he is the most beloved living songwriter would be

selling him short somehow. Because for a lot of people he is also their favorite person.

John Prine's latest gift to Americana, country, and roots music has been his support of the next generation of singer-songwriters, including Sturgill Simpson, Chris Stapleton, Dan Auerbach, Margo Price, Jason Isabell, Amanda Shires, Brandi Carlile, and Kacey Musgraves. Prine's backing of young musicians involves offering suggestions and invitations to his house, and recording and performing with them. In an article from *Nashville Scene* magazine, Sturgill Simpson gratefully acknowledges John Prine's guidance:

> "No matter what I could say, it would never capture the love and admiration and gratitude I feel in my heart for him. There is no other and there will never be another John Prine. He has no idea, but he has always been the coolest guy in the room his entire life. I think a great deal of that is because he really listens. He's always listening, processing. He has at times given me some of the best advice I've ever had from anyone, but the times I've probably learned the most from him was sitting in a room when he didn't say anything at all."

Artists Who Influenced John Prine

Bob Dylan, Roger Williams, Willie Nelson, Hank Williams, Johnny Cash, and Ramblin' Jack Elliot.

Americana Artists Influenced by John Prine

John Mellencamp, Steve Earle, Lilly Hiatt, Aaron Lee Tasjan, Chris Knight, Bill Morrissey, James McMurtry, Monte Warden, Charlie Robison, Sturgill Simpson, Amanda Shires, Jason Isabell, Margo Price, Brandi Carlile, and Mike Plume.

Following Their Footsteps

Inspired by the music of the trailblazers and embodying those traits associated with Americana music, these nine disciples have become pioneers themselves, influencing current and future Americana artists.

Beachwood Sparks

If Gram Parsons were alive today, Beachwood Sparks would be his favorite band. No group has emulated the Cosmic American sound of Parsons' Flying Burrito Brothers with the same honesty, passion, and originality as has this Los Angeles alt-country outfit, led on their first two albums by bassist Brent Rademaker, drummer Aaron Sperske, and guitarists Chris Gunst and Dave Scher.

In 2000 Beachwood Sparks released their self-titled debut album, *Beachwood Sparks*, and immediately reviewers took note of the band's influences. From a 2009 article titled "Beachwood Sparks: An L.A. Story, Past & Present," the record is portrayed as "an accomplished, totally enjoyable slice of Laurel canyon rock that sounds as fresh today as it did nine years ago. Heavily influenced by *The Notorious Byrd Brothers*, it would have had a really good shot at the charts in 1968 or 2008 (the year of Fleet Foxes). The band was making Cosmic American music at a time when not many of their contemporaries were doing it." Stephen M. Deusner, writing in *Pitchfork* magazine, found the band "steeping themselves in [the music of] Gram Parsons, Buffalo Springfield, and *Bradley's Barn*-era Beau Brummels." Another critic, commenting in thecalmingseas.com, would describe Beachwood Sparks' sound as "country through a kaleidoscope." And in an interview with Andrew Lindsay, Neal Casal, formerly of Ryan Adams & the Cardinals, lists *Beachwood Sparks* among his all-time favorite albums.

Beachwood Sparks add psychedelic atmospherics and trippy lyrics to a jangling, twangy, country-rock foundation in all 14 tracks. Many of the song titles themselves ("Ballad of Never Rider," "Singing Butterfly," "This Is What It Feels Like") preface the surreal and calming musical textures that follow. "Desert Skies," "The Calming Seas," "Sleeping Butterfly," and "Canyon Ride" illustrate the record's recurring theme of escape through nature. True to their influences, at times it seems as if Sneaky Pete is behind the pedal steel and that Roger McGuinn is playing his twelve-string Rickenbacker.

On the subject of Cosmic American Music, columnist Laura Snapes, writing in the *Guardian*, in an interview with William Tyler, past member of Lambchop and Silver Jews, seeks to find a distinction between Cosmic American and Americana. Tyler had this to say: "I love the term Americana, but I feel like, when you put the 'cosmic' on it, it's about connecting psychedelic and exploratory music to traditional American roots music, which you can trace from the Grateful Dead through Los Lobos, Wilco, Yo La Tengo and Lambchop."

A more thorough definition of Cosmic American Music than the one found in a column from *No Depression* magazine on March 21, 2018 would be difficult to find. The author first plucks quotes from a Michael Grimshaw essay, "Redneck Religion and Shitkickin' Saviours? Gram

Parsons, Theology and Country Music," before offering his own:

> "Parsons' mission [according to Grimshaw] was the creation of a new way to musically heal the separation and increasing divisiveness of late modern life. His term for what he attempted was Cosmic American Music... To do so, Parsons reused the language and rhythms of rock, and in himself attempted the incarnated embodiment of a musical and cultural reconciliation. To speak theologically he was both prophet and messiah; both pointing the way to a new beginning and attempting to live out the struggles of just what that new beginning involved."

Now, a portion of the columnist's own definition:

> [Cosmic American Music] is not pure country in the sense of it being solely traditional or "trad." It is usually more closely aligned with Bakersfield than Appalachian, though incorporates diverse background elements, including rock, soul, and jazz... It is not usually "Outlaw" as epitomized by those who have recently co-opted that label; having said that, in some ways it followed Hank and Cash as the original outlaws of country music... There is a large West Coast/Californian aspect to it. .. It's not soul music per se, though Gram once described it as "white soul," and it is usually soulful in some way... Above all Cosmic American Music is inventive in

songwriting and delivery, cosmic in the sense of being cutting edge, but built upon the tried and true (e.g., Buck Owens, Merle Haggard, Louvin Brothers, Elvis).

Pastoral imagery conveyed through haunting harmonies backed by shimmering guitars, a dizzy pedal steel, and an ethereal organ, the next album set out to explore more psychedelic-country pathways. A year later (2001), Beachwood Sparks released what many believe to be their seminal work, *Once We Were Trees*, and once more "their four-part harmonies soar to meet that now familiar Westcoast jangle, tart pop songs blending into a deep rich mulch out of which melodies grow like wildflowers," as Raoul Hernandez wrote in *The Austin Chronicle*. Reviewer Yancey Stricker, from Neumu.net, noted the group's indebtedness to another band: "The majority of the songs feature a tight country-rock sound with subtle harmonies and a great feel for melody. The Beachwood Sparks balance deft restraint with hot guitar licks, making *Once We Were Trees* the best Byrds album since *Sweetheart of the Rodeo*."

A signature of Beachwood Sparks, the quirky song titles ("Once We Were Trees," "Banjo Press Conference," "Juggler's Revenge") belie the steady excellence of the musicianship, especially found in the dreamy, mellow tracks ("Hearts Mend," "Let It Run," "Old Manatee," "Close Your Eyes," "The Good Night Whistle).

True to their country-rock roots yet blissfully original, Beachwood Sparks are proof that psychedelia and country when mixed make for a tantalizing musical cocktail well worth sipping and a drink that Gram Parsons would no doubt wish to sample.

Mary Chapin Carpenter

Beachwood Sparks is as little known as the next trailblazing disciple is recognized. Country Music Association (CMA) Female Vocalist of the Year (1992, 1993), inducted into the Nashville Songwriters Hall of Fame in 2012, winner of five Grammys and the 2010 "Spirit of Americana" Free Speech Award, singer-songwriter Mary Chapin Carpenter encapsulates the introspective, folk-inspired artist. A Washington D.C. coffeehouse folk singer with an Ivy League degree from Brown University seems an unlikely backstory for a future (for a while anyway) country music star. As difficult to place into a musical slot as any artist, Mary Chapin Carpenter's genre-blurring style probably fits the Americana moniker best.

    Of the nine disciples listed in this chapter, Mary Chapin Carpenter's name is the most recognizable. Although many of Americana's artists often work in relative obscurity, Chapin is an example of the Americana performer whose talents are appreciated worldwide. Three albums (*Come On Come On*, *Stones in the Road*, *The Age of Miracles*) from the thirteen studio LPs she has released reveal why.

    Come On Come On (1992) dominated the *Billboard* Hot Country Songs chart—"I Feel Lucky" (#4), "Not Too Much to Ask" with Joe Diffie (#15), "Passionate Kisses" (#4), "The Hard Way" (#11), "The Bug" (#16), "He Thinks He'll Keep Her" (#2), and "I Take My Chances" (#1). For the year, the album itself finished #6 on the *Billboard* country album chart. Unlike most of the mainstream country music of the early 1990s through today, the lyrics on this record offered "a thoroughly modern take on what comprised country music," writes Holly Gleason in *American Songwriter*. Gleason calls "The Hard Way" "a Rickenbacker-drenched, post-feminist anthem about the price paid for the ground gained personally as well as sociologically." Chapin addresses the pain of divorce on "Only a Dream"; carnal desire in "I Feel Lucky" and "Passionate Kisses"; and small town America in "I Am a Town" with a poignancy and lyrical brilliance rarely heard on country pop stations. With *Come On Come On*, Mary Chapin Carpenter began to gain momentum with listeners who previously were not part of country music's demographics. As Gleason explains:

> For Carpenter, the silken arrangements, Beatles and Byrds jangle guitar flourishes and knowing ability to make the (upper) middle class common offered a signature of American evolution. Country wasn't rural; it was anyone who could see themselves in the songs—and for NPR listeners, college students, women carpooling and holding jobs, people falling in love and apart, this was the music of their life. And what lives they were.

Americana artists, by definition, enjoy a broad spectrum of musical tastes. Mary Chapin Carpenter, in an article titled "This Music Made Me," listed the ten albums that influenced her the most. In addition to linking these recordings with her own, Carpenter's reflections provide a passage into the mind of a gifted singer-songwriter. Here are a few of Carpenter's choices along with her thoughts:

> The Beatles/*Sgt. Pepper's Lonely Hearts Club Band*: What can be said about this life-changing record? It's already been said, and I will simply add that in truth every Beatles record could be on this list alongside this one. Bob Dylan/*Blood on the Tracks*: I think I

played this album every day of every month. I think that the records you love during that time in your life stay with you forever. The Band/*The Band*: Every song on the album kills me. The Band were incredibly important to me as I was growing up. They had such a handmade quality to what they did, but it was never precious or frail, just utterly original. Jackson Browne/*Jackson Browne*: Intelligent, musical, hit bound. This was California to me long before I ever got there. Joni Mitchell/*Hejira*: Songs of love and travel, mystical and life transforming. Joni Mitchell has been such an enormous artistic influence on so many artists, it's almost impossible to overstate it. I think she is a genius, as a writer, a player, and a creative force.

Mary Chapin Carpenter's next studio release, *Stones in the Road* (1994), became *Billboard's* #1 Country Album of the Year. The LP produced four hit singles, including a #1 with "Shut Up and Kiss Me." More folk-inspired and introspective than *Come On Come On*, the record marks a high point in Carpenter's artistic craftsmanship. The uncluttered arrangements, literate lyrics, and melodic vocals combine to produce an album that is nothing short of astonishing. Songs of unusual emotional depth include "House of Cards," "Stones in the Road," "The End of My Pirate Days," "John Doe No. 24," "Jubilee," "Outside Looking In," and "This Is Love."

Sputnikmusic.com in 2017 assessed Mary Chapin Carpenter's singer-songwriter expertise on *Stones* with these words:

> In the end, just as Carpenter can balance genres to achieve a unique but instantly recognizable sound, she also harnesses somber and lightweight emotions to achieve a yin-and-yang combination that allows honesty to bleed through that any listener can relate, perhaps most evidently in the album's closer, "This Is Love." This balance is not only her most powerful skill as a musician, but something that allows the album to live outside its respective genres and exist as a truly singular work that deserves just as much recognition now as it did when it first graced the Earth in 1994.

2010 saw Mary Chapin Carpenter returning to the successful formula that produced *Come On Come On* and *Stones in the Road* with *The Age of Miracles* but without the support of mainstream Nashville. Carpenter by now had left a market-driven establishment only interested in finding singles to land on country radio. Her dissatisfaction with the "corporate" country music might be found in her remarks about the topic of musical artists being allowed to express political opinions. Responding to the "Shut up and sing" verbal stance against the Dixie Chicks and others, Carpenter, who has never shied away from sharing her personal beliefs, told *Rolling Stone's* Stephen L. Betts:

> That's so offensive to me. What? I'm not allowed to have a brain? I'm not allowed to speak to issues that affect me? They affect all of us. I don't subscribe to that way of thinking. I never have and I never will. How can I write songs about life if I'm not experiencing it and forming opinions and having opinions and advocating on behalf of

things that are important to me? I just never felt any other way about it. People who are dismissive or critical—or at worst, hateful of artists who speak out or who choose to align themselves with a particular viewpoint or cause, I didn't ever think that wanting to be an artist would preclude me from having an opinion. I mean, I don't sing about flowers.

The Age of Miracles displays the Mary Chapin Carpenter stamp of excellence: tight musicianship, pitch-perfect vocals, and evocative lyrics. On this album Carpenter gets help from Allison Krauss and Vince Gill on background vocals and Russ Kunkel on drums. Interestingly, *Miracles* debuted within the top ten of the *Billboard* Top Rock Albums chart and peaked at number one on the Folk Music chart. Finding a specific category for her music has always proved challenging. The album, with no singles charting on the *Billboard* Hot Country Songs list, still managed to reach number six on the *Billboard* Top Country Albums chart. Carpenter was gaining a wider audience, and yet many of her earlier fans apparently did not mind the increased introspection found on more recent albums.

With the exception of the "The Way I Feel," most of the subject material reveals a pensive narrator. Reviewer Peggy Fry states that with *The Age of Miracles*, Mary Chapin Carpenter returns to the road, literally and figuratively. [It is a record] that builds on her core theme: the never-ending journey within and without, in search of that perfect intersection where our private and mutual dreams and fears are held in precarious, delicate balance." Fry's insights are best realized in "The Age of Miracles," "We Traveled So Far," "Mrs. Hemingway," "Holding up the Sky," and "Zephyr." In each of these soul-searching, discerning meditations about the challenges we must face in this life, Mary Chapin Carpenter offers clarity and, above all else, comfort. There is something mysteriously captivating about the way in which Carpenter, in this album and others, touches the listener's heart and mind so naturally.

Today, Mary Chapin Carpenter is recognized mostly as an Americana artist, and she seems at peace with that label. Speaking with author Michael Scott Cain, Mary Chapin Carpenter shared her views on Americana music:

> "What exactly is Americana? That's a question that has no answer. Music was never so compartmentalized as it was in the nineties. Everything was genre, and every radio station was carefully formatted. Americana broke that up. Now it includes blues, rock, country, folk, everything that has a base in roots music. That said, it's an umbrella term for anything that has a roots quality. . . It's [Americana's] very freeing. Why wouldn't I want to be associated with a form that allows me to be outside a box?"

Carpenter's allegiance to roots music and as a singer-songwriter who follows her own musical vision instead of a market-driven path places her among the most important and influential Americana artists.

Rodney Crowell

Former member of Emmylou Harris' Hot Band, singer-songwriter Rodney Crowell would leave the world of mainstream country (where he enjoyed great success) to pursue a musical vision closer to his core being, nearer to his heart, conscience, and creative urges. In the process he would construct a songwriting template of exceptional, perhaps unmatched, artistry.

Author Michael Steissguth, in his book *Outlaw: Waylon, Willie, Kris, and the Renegades of Nashville*, traces the musical path that eventually led Houston-born Crowell to Nashville in 1972. As Steissgurth writes: "In what became one of Nashville's great hungry-artist stories, Crowell slept in his car amid the musty aroma of sumac trees, bathed in lakes outside town until the weather turned cold, and poked around the West End meeting songwriters." Here he met up with two of his greatest influences, singer-songwriters Guy Clark and Townes Van Zandt.

Fast forwarding to 1975, Emmylou Harris, who had recorded Crowell's "Bluebird Wine" on her *Pieces of the Sky* album, invited him to join her Hot Band as rhythm guitarist and vocalist. Crowell continued writing songs and after leaving the Hot Band released his first solo LP, *Ain't Living Long Like This*. Crowell was more successful as a songwriter than as a solo artist with Johnny Cash, Waylon Jennings, Jerry Reed, Rosanne Cash and other country stars recording his songs. Crowell had to wait until 1988 before he gained any traction as a recording artist with the release of the critically-acclaimed *Diamonds in the Dirt*, an album that produced an astounding five #1 singles: "It's Such a Small World" (with Roseanne Cash), "I Couldn't Leave You If I Tried," "She's Crazy For Leavin'," "After All This Time," and Buck Owens cover "Above and Beyond." Rodney Crowell's follow-up album, *Keys to the Highway* (1989), like *Diamonds*, sold well. Only one of Crowell's next three studio releases, however, would find room on the *Billboard* Top Country Albums chart, prompting him to shift his musical vision from country mainstream to a more folk, country-rock, Americana ethos as Rodney Crowell's next three releases—*The Houston Kid* (2001), *Fate's Right Hand* (2003), and *The Outsider* (2005)—boldly announced.

In a 2001 interview with *Billboard* magazine, Rodney Crowell shared the following reflections about *The Houston Kid*: "I feel like it's Americana music with a kind of folk underpinning. No way this gets played on country radio. But it does have the sensibility country comes from—and the traditions of country music, like honesty and storytelling." The autobiographical album, as Crowell stated, "Takes my experiences from 6 to 15 years old, and it sort of cross-pollinates with other kids in my neighborhood. It fuses their experiences with what was going on in my life [in East Houston]." Crowell was correct. The subject matter explored in the songs would prohibit their being played on country mainstream radio: AIDS ("I Wish It Would Rain"), bisexuality ("Wandering Boy"), alcohol abuse and father-son conflicts ("The Rock of My Soul"), and domestic violence ("Topsy Turvy"). Crowell expressed pleasure with the result: "I feel like this is the first time I could walk away from making a record with all my self-respect." His musical integrity was intact.

Less darkly-lit tracks include "I Walk the Line Revisited," a cheerful duet with former father-in-law, Johnny Cash; "Telephone Road," a rocker depicting fond childhood memories; "Why Don't We Talk About It," an upbeat look at love's second-chances; and "I Know Love Is All You Need," a contemplation on the healing power of redemption.

With his next release, *Fate's Right Hand*, Rodney Crowell's compositions centered on topics related to middle age rather than memories as he told country music journalist Edward Morris:

> "[The new album] is more me in that it's me trying to make sense of the right now. *The Houston Kid* was based on true things that happened. But I know—from writing a memoir that I've been working on for a

while—that reconstructing memory is revisionism. It is by nature, because if you're any kind of poet when you start reconstructing the past, you're going to add to it a little bit. This record is about finding poetry in the actual middle of the activity."

As expected, all eleven tracks were written by Rodney Crowell. "Still Learning How to Fly," a spirited anthem about living in the moment, appropriately sets the tone for an album whose voice speaks through middle-age sensibilities. In "Earthbound" Crowell finds solace in naming those individuals whose lives echo his own (Aretha Franklin, Seamus Heaney, Ringo Starr, Dalai Lama, among others). "Time to Go Inward" relates Crowell's search for spiritual wisdom while "The Man in Me" sees Crowell angrily exposing the hypocrite in himself. As with Mary Chapin Carpenter, Rodney Crowell does not hesitate to offer political commentary. On "It's a Different World Now," the subjects of Crowell's angst include environmental recklessness, military imperialism, and moral abandonment.

From the Edmond Morris article, a final perspective on *Fate's Right Hand*: "Fame is for the young, and Crowell's been through all that. *Fate's Right Hand* celebrates wisdom's more enduring gold. 'Our culture aggrandizes youth ad nauseam,' he says. 'I'm hoping that there's a window in our culture where the truth about the middle of your life matters. And it ain't easy. I can't tell anybody anything, but I can show them what's up for me and hope it rings true.'"

The next studio release, *The Outsider*, completes Rodney Crowell's trailblazing album trilogy begun with *The Houston Kid* and followed by *Fate's Right Hand*. Where the first record reviewed his youth and the second shared his metaphysics, *The Outsider* explored Crowell's political and social consciousness. "Don't Get Me Started" angrily protests the war in Iraq; "The Obscenity Prayer" lashes out at the political right's sense of privilege; "We Can't Turn Back Now" pleads for tolerance; and "Ignorance Is the Enemy," featuring the speaking voices of Emmylou Harris and John Prine, tenderly conveys this maxim.

The Outsider is not entirely devoted to hearing Crowell's political manifesto as the groove-gorged, country-rocker "Say You Love Me" and the velvety, harmonious "Glasgow Girl" testify. In the former, the carnal desires of the narrator are intensified by Crowell's mastery of the musical hook; conversely, the narrator in the latter unveils a poetic enchantment of the woman.

Rodney Crowell's intrepid decision to explore a musical road not built by Music Row reveals the integrity, tenacity, and talent of an Americana trailblazer. Not that he would care, Crowell probably will not earn any more CMA nominations or awards. Winning seven from the Americana Music Association (AMA), including the 2006 Lifetime Achievement Award in Songwriting, probably means a great deal more.

Iris DeMent

Blessed with a gospel-tinged, riveting voice and church-pulpit earnestness, Iris DeMent's reflections on family, religion and politics immediately transport the listener. Recipient of the Americana Trailblazer Award in 2017, Iris DeMent has carved out a unique niche among Americana artists, most markedly on three albums—*Infamous Angel* (1992), *My Life* (1993), and *Sing the Delta* (2012).

Iris DeMent's Arkansas roots, Pentecostal background, and being one of fourteen children has profoundly shaped her music, especially in her debut LP,

Infamous Angel. "Our Town," "Let the Mystery Be," "Mama's Opry," "After You're Gone," "These Hills," "Infamous Angel," and "Higher Ground" (where her mother sings lead) simply and sweetly celebrate rural themes: tradition, faith, family, and love. DeMent's soprano, rare and rapturous, reawakens an earlier time, when the Carter Family famously delivered universal truths in a gospel, bluegrass, country style as has DeMent.

On the topic of faith, in "Let the Mystery Be," one of DeMent's most-acclaimed compositions, she reveals her skepticism of religion yet acknowledges the key role it has played in her life and music, as she reflects in a 2012 NPR interview:

> "It [our home] was full gospel fundamentalist, I guess you'd call it. There was hell and there was heaven, and the in-between was just kind of preparation to get to the better place. In everyday life, your primary focus was staying out of the bottom side of the afterlife. I have zero regrets about having been brought up that way—in fact, I can't even put into words how grateful I am for it. There were some useless things and some, I suppose, somewhat damaging things that I got from it. But . . . there was sincerity in there, as well, and a really good message that came through about what's going on underneath the waters of life. My parents just gave me a gift I can't even put a finger on. . . My mom, who sang straight up until the day she died, told me one day: 'You know, Iris, singing. There ain't no difference.' So I think, even though I've left the church and moved away from a lot of things that didn't do me any good, I continued to pray—and

that is singing for me. That's as close as I get to praying."

Alanna Nash, reviewing Iris DeMent's next release, *My Life*, states, "No average country troubadour, DeMent is a backwoods Emily Dickinson." When compared with *Infamous Angel*, "*My Life* is more like a diary, a bittersweet collection of fist-clenched confessions," says David Okamoto of *Rolling Stone* magazine. DeMent writes about the following: the inability to grieve her father's death ("No Time to Cry"); the effects of a loveless marriage ("Easy's Getting Harder Every Day"); and an apology to a former lover ("You've Done Nothing Wrong"). The acoustic instrumentation, featuring some of the finest pickers in the business (Al Perkins/dobro, Stuart Duncan/fiddle), perfectly complements the pure vocals and moving lyrics.

    Iris DeMent had not released an album of original material for sixteen years until *Sing the Delta* came out in 2012. The Delta, in this instance, is the Arkansas Delta where her family, faith, and musical roots took shape as echoed in the plainspoken, rural South vernacular that inhabits her soaring voice. The album celebrates those childhood memories and country values DeMent still holds dear ("Mama Was Always Tellin' Her Truth," "Sing the Delta," "If That Ain't Love," "Makin' My Way Back Home"), but other tracks show DeMent questioning (artfully) the evangelical beliefs she was taught to accept as Jonathan Keefe from *Slant* magazine points out:

> DeMent's complicated relationship with her religious upbringing, in particular, has always figured prominently in her work, and those issues continue to drive much of *Sing the Delta*. Each of the songs on the album is structured as a hymn in the Southern gospel tradition, and most of DeMent and co-

producer Bo Ramsey's arrangements are grounded in DeMent's spirited church-piano style playing. The use of these conservative conventions is ultimately a smart, subversive production choice, as they play against DeMent's challenges to traditional religious tenets on songs like "The Kingdom Has Already Come" and the stunning album closer "Out of the Fire."

Two more songs, "The Night I Learned How Not to Pray" and "There's a Whole Lot of Heaven," poignantly make known DeMent's faith struggles as well.

Iris DeMent singles out a central tenet found in the Americana singer-songwriter ethos in the following excerpt from her interview with Jewly Hight of *American Songwriter* magazine. DeMent was asked what she thought her career would be like after arriving in Nashville for the first time:

> You know, I realize looking back I thought it would be like this. I mean, I got the call to write and sing. I knew that. I didn't get the call to sell millions of records. The voice didn't say, "Hey Iris, you're gonna be a star." I didn't hear that voice. . . All I knew was I was told to do music, to write and sing for people. If fifteen people hear it, if five hundred thousand people hear it, that's really not my concern. Never was. It still isn't. I feel like when I make a record, I love it and I care about it. I want people to hear it. But if I do my job and nobody does, I will sleep fine with that.

Few can claim to be as authentically Americana as Iris DeMent. Indeed, many have crowned her "Queen of Americana," a title perhaps only Emmylou Harris could herald as her own.

Steve Earle

A prolific singer-songwriter whose songs have been recorded by Carl Perkins, Travis Tritt, Johnny Cash, Patty Loveless, Waylon Jennings, Vince Gill, Shawn Colvin, and Emmylou Harris, trailblazer Steve Earle, a three-time Grammy winner and the 2004 "Spirit of Americana" Free Speech Award winner, has made a lasting impression on folk, country, country rock, outlaw country, roots rock and Americana with his indefatigable and intrepid spirit of musical adventure.

Like Rodney Crowell, Steve Earle first made an impression as a Nashville songwriter with some success before becoming a well-known singer. Going back and forth to Music City from his San Antonio home, Earle eventually brought the band he formed in Texas, the Dukes, to Nashville in 1986 and recorded *Guitar Town*, a critically-acclaimed debut LP of enormous influence that hit #1 on the *Billboard* Top Country Album chart. As *Rolling Stone* magazine states in its "100 Best Albums of the Eighties" list:

> When Earle finally did get to make a full-length album in 1986, after writing songs for artists ranging from Waylon Jennings to Carl Perkins, he could apply professional polish to his Dylanesque verse and outlaw style of music. The result was *Guitar Town*, an album that straddled country and rock to create

something startling new. In the words of a fellow artist, John Hiatt, it was "pretty much a darn near flawless record. Great writing, fantastic album."

Pugnacious, rebellious, edgy, *Guitar Town* twanged and rocked as hard and honestly as any country-rock album before or since in "Guitar Town," "Good Ol' Boy (Getting' Tough)," and "Someday." Steve Earle offers rockabilly ("Think It Over," "Hillbilly Highway"), country folk ("Little Rock 'n' Roller"), country blues ("My Old Friend the Blues"), and progressive bluegrass ("Down the Road"). The trim production and tasty musicianship along with the unsentimental, frank, and well-crafted lyrics produced a record possessing the enduring traits of a classic.

Although Steve Earle's next release, *Exit 0* (1987), earned mostly favorable reviews, the album, understandably, had trouble matching the almost unanimous affection for *Guitar Town*. It did include one of Earle's greatest songs, "Nowhere Road," which received a Grammy nomination for Best Country Song. With his third studio album, *Copperhead Road* (1988), Earle unleashes, on the record's first side, a fierce combination of hard rock and country in "Copperhead Road," "Snake Oil," "Back to the Wall," and "The Devil's Right Hand," dealing out vivid drug references and emotionally scarred Vietnam vets. Earle forgoes the angry tone on side two to deliver some of the most touching love songs he's written: "You Belong to Me," "Even When I'm Blue," "Waiting on You," and "Once You Love."

Looking back on *Copperhead Road* from a distance of thirty years in a 2018 interview with Joshua Miller, Steve Earle shared these observations about the LP:

"It was sort of obvious that country music had decided that I didn't belong, and I had to find another place to go. So, I started finding ways to get on rock radio. I needed to get played somewhere else in order to keep having a career. I wanted to do enough that I didn't have to get a job. It's an important record to me because I felt I had to make that record the way I wanted to make it. I saw it as an escape from the demise of my career rather than continue to make country records for radio."

Steve Earle's descent into heroin addiction, jail time, and marital failures in the late 1980s and early 1990s have been well documented. Thankfully, drug treatment was effective in saving his life and recharging his creative batteries as his 1995 acoustic gem, *Train a Comin'* confirms. Once again Earle demonstrates an incomparable grasp of a wide range of musical styles as evidenced by his graceful command of traditional folk and bluegrass on this recording. Only four artists, including Emmylou Harris, assisted Earle, drawing production parallels to Dylan's *John Wesley Harding* and *Nashville Skyline*. Except for covers of Townes Van Zandt's "Tecumseh Valley," the Beatles' "I'm Looking Through You," the Melodians' "Rivers of Babylon," and Norman Blake's instrumental "Northern Winds," all the tracks were written by Earle.

USA Today named *Train a Comin'* as its top choice for country music album of the year, a decision writer Eric Dennis might sanction as his words suggest:

> As curious or as charming as they may be these covers pale in comparison to Earle's own material on *Train*, all of which is acoustic and most of which splits evenly between regret-tinged love songs and historically-influenced tales of war and

> violence. For all his gruffness and rough edges, Earle has always been capable of writing tender songs like a true balladeer... One of Earle's greatest traits has long been his ability to evoke specific locales and characters from the past with a large degree of authenticity, and it's in this geography where *Train a Comin's* real masterpiece can be found.

Clean and sober now, Steve Earle enjoyed his most prolific recording period, producing one excellent album after another. Of Earle's sixteen studio releases, *El Corazon* (1997) just may be his crowning achievement. With his previous album, *I Feel Alright* (1996), Earle, accompanied by the Dukes, left behind the sparse, acoustically-driven musical landscape of *Train a Comin'* and triumphantly revived (mostly) the original outlaw, country-rock style that he pioneered with his first records. The same can be said of *El Corazon*, except that Earle's musical eclecticism spreads further. There is alt-country, "Here I Am" and "Poison Lovers"; bluegrass, "I Still Carry You Around" and "You Know the Rest," featuring the Del McCoury Band, with whom Earle later would record the highly-acclaimed *The Mountain* (1998); traditional country, "The Other Side of Town"; R&B, "Telephone Road"; the ballad, "Christmas in Washington" and "Ft. Worth Blues"; roots rock, "Somewhere Out There"; and hard rock, "Taneytown," "If You Fall" and "N.Y.C." Also worth mentioning are the strong duets with Emmylou Harris ("Tanneytown") and Siobhan Kennedy ("Poison Lovers"), two of many duets that Steve Earle has popularized over the years.

The pioneering musical force that is Steve Earle is summed up well by Grant Alden, who, writing in *No Depression* magazine, believes Steve Earle to possess "a continuing instinct for unflinching courage as songwriter, observer, and performer. . . [with an] unquenchable joy in making music . . . his is a uniquely American voice, and both thematically and musically he is able to reach down and squeeze hard the core of our synthetic American soul. Kinda like CPR for Music Row, y'know?"

Steve Earle has credited Guy Clark and Townes Van Zandt as his two greatest influences, but Earle took inspiration from trailblazers Dylan, Parsons, and Prine. According to inflooenz.com, Earle also has inspired many artists, leading a roster of disciples (Gill Landry, Chris Knight, Josh Abbot Band, Robbie Fulks, and the Backsliders, to name of few) that continues to swell over time.

Emmylou Harris

Gram Parsons' most famous disciple, Country Music Hall of Fame inductee, winner of fourteen Grammy Awards including the Grammy Lifetime Achievement Award, and recipient of additional honors and awards too numerous to list, Emmylou Harris is, without question, the face of Americana music. No current Americana artist boasts as rich a discography: twenty-six studio albums, three live albums, eleven compilation albums, and seventy singles. Harris has recorded with Americana trailblazers Gram Parsons, Bob Dylan, the Band, and John Prine. Add Willie Nelson, Neil Young, Roy Orbison, and Rodney Crowell, among others, to this remarkable roster. Emmylou Harris' impact on contemporary music has been profound.

During her early folk-singing days, Emmylou Harris struggled for a while with poverty following a number of personal crises, including a broken marriage leading to single motherhood and her first record label declaring bankruptcy. Good fortune eventually smiled upon Harris as the well-known account reads, when Chris Hillman of the Flying Burrito Brothers saw her sing as part of a trio in a Washington D.C. club. Although Gram Parsons had already left the Burritos, Hillman, quite perceptively as it turned out, later recommended her to Parsons, who was beginning a solo career. Parsons took Harris under his wing and the rest, as the saying goes, is history. Their harmonies on *GP*, *Grievous Angel*, and the Fallen Angels tour were magical from the beginning. Harris never tires of describing Gram Parsons' influence on her music, as she told interviewer Daiana Feuer:

> "Gram was the beginning for me. Yes, there were other things like folk music—Bob Dylan and Joan Baez got me to pick up a guitar and learn songs and sing. But I found whatever voice I have, that is, if there's any authenticity at all, it came from singing harmonies with Gram—working with him, simplifying what I was doing, bringing that soulfulness of country music. I was born in Alabama but I was raised on military bases. Music didn't have hold on me until folk music came around in the 1960s, and it came to a peak working with Gram. I owe him so much. He helped me find my voice. That is a fact that will never change."

After Gram Parsons' tragic death at 26 due to a drug overdose, Harris dealt with her grief by throwing herself into work and quickly formed a band (the Hot Band), primarily made up of musicians who played on her 1975 major label debut album, *Pieces of the Sky*. As talented a collection of musicians as any artist is likely to put together, Harris' Hot Band included legendary guitarist James Burton, who had played with Gram Parsons, Elvis Presley, and Ricky Nelson; pianist Glen Hardin, who also had backed Parsons and Presley; and singer-songwriter Rodney Crowell, who was asked to play rhythm guitar and lend vocals. Fiddle and mandolin master, Byron Berline; Neil Young's gifted pedal steel guitarist, Ben Keith; celebrated singer Linda Ronstadt; former Burrito and Eagle, multi-instrumentalist Bernie Leadon; sublime vocalist and banjoist Herb Pedersen; and another fiddler of repute, Ricky Skaggs, appear on the release.

Pieces of the Sky's eclectic song list, dominated by covers of country hits, offered something for everybody: a *Billboard* country hit (#4) with a Louvin Brothers song, "If I Could Only Win Your Love"; a Harris-penned grieving reflection enkindled by Parsons' death, "Boulder to Birmingham," a gospel-tinged track covered by many artists including the Hollies, Dolly Parton, and Joan Baez; a Beatles tune, "For No One"; a song she and Parsons recorded and regularly performed live, the Bryant-duo heartbreak gem, "Sleepless Nights," performed later by Norah Jones, Elvis Costello, Eddie Vedder, Albert Lee, the Judds, Patty Loveless, and Lucinda Williams; Dolly Parton's autobiographical country classic, "Coat of Many Colors"; a couple of drinking cuts, Rodney Crowell's "Bluebird Wine" and Merle Haggard's "Bottle Let Me Down"; Billy Sherrill's touching love ballad, "Too Far Gone"; Danny Flowers' heart-rending "Before Believing"; and Shell Silverstein's honky-tonk jewel, "Queen of the Silver Dollar."

What distinguished this recording from the mainstream country albums released at the time was Emmylou Harris' knack at choosing songs that fit the Cosmic-American musical vernacular mentor Gram Parsons had instructed her in so well. In particular, Herb Pedersen and Emmylou Harris' spirited and tight harmonies smoothly link this recording to Harris' fabled duets with Parsons, in the process making the old-time hits sound new again and helping the LP to reach #7 on the 1975 *Billboard* country album chart. Looking back on *Pieces*, Emmylou Harris told interviewer Bud Scoppa:

> "I thought the closest I could get to Gram would be through the people he worked with. Then Brian [Ahern, the producer] signed Rodney Crowell, so all the other pieces started to come together. It was a beautiful mixing of a cosmic stew. Keeping Gram's music alive was what I thought my purpose was. I didn't understand why the whole world wasn't crying out like I was at the loss of Gram. Also, he had affected me so much on an artistic level, I felt like I had to give it to others the way it had been given to me. It's strange how emotions work, but there was something valid there. It's the way we deal with what comes through us; we have to plow it under and make something out of it."

Emmylou Harris' next release, *Elite Hotel* (1975) and the one that followed, *Luxury Liner* (1976), stayed with the eclectic, cosmic-country sounds found on *Pieces of the Sky*. Indeed, *Elite Hotel* surpassed *Pieces* by placing #1 on the *Billboard* country album chart. Three singles also scored big—"Together Again" (#1), "Sweet Dreams" (#1), and "One of these Days" (#3). Harris pays homage to her former tutor, Gram Parsons, by singing three of his songs—"Sin City," "Wheels," and "Ooh Las Vegas." Emmylou Harris' most commercially successful recording streak continued with *Luxury Liner*, which reached #3 on the *Billboard* country album chart and produced two hit singles—"(You Never Can Tell) C'est la Vie" (#6) and "Making Believe."

Gram Parsons' "Luxury Liner" and "She" were also covered.

Both records were built around a voice that was growing more confident and fresh interpretations of country classics that introduced a new generation to the great songwriters from country music's hallowed past (Buck Owens, Don Gibson, Hank Williams, Wayne Kemp, Ira and Charlie Louvin, and A.P. Carter). Awakening listeners to the wonderful songs of the past remains one of Emmylou Harris' most enduring gifts to contemporary music. But Harris also saw to it to display the merits of current songwriters Rodney Crowell ("Amarillo", "Till I Gain Control Again," "You're Supposed to Be Feeling Good," and "Tulsa Queen"), Susanna Clark (I'll Be Your San Antone Rose"), and Townes Van Zandt ("Pancho and Lefty").

Emmylou Harris' next LP, *Quarter Moon in a Ten Cent Town* (1978), climbed to #3 on the *Billboard* country album chart and included three hit singles: "To Daddy" (#3), "Two More Bottles of Wine" (#1), and "Easy from Now On" (#12). Unlike the previous three works, instead of relying on a country-rock sound, a more traditional-country style begins to emerge. Quite interesting are the additions to the studio personnel this time around: the Band's Rick Danko and Garth Hudson, and also Willie Nelson, who duets with her on "One Paper Kid." Two albums later, Emmylou Harris would risk upsetting her fan base and record sales by taking a dip in the waters of bluegrass with the 1980 release of *Roses in the Snow*.

Harris shared these comments about *Roses in the Snow* to Bud Scoppa:

> "Back then [1980], everybody was drinking from the bluegrass cup, including Linda Ronstadt, but nobody was recording it. So a certain ego [the born leader trait?] in me said,

"I've got Ricky Skaggs in the band now, and it's going on anyway, so it's crazy not to do a bluegrass.' Instead of going backwards into 'son of *Elite Hotel*,' which we thought the record company wanted we decide to make a bluegrass record with some serious pickers. I thought the record would be a commercial disaster, but I was arrogant enough at that point in my career and in my youth that I could sustain such a disaster; it was more important to follow my artistic path. When it became a Top 10 hit, I was patting myself on the back for following my convictions, and figuring that was how it would always be— and then I made *The Ballad of Sally Rose* and almost went bankrupt. So you live and learn."

In this single paragraph Emmylou Harris distills the Americana musician's pursuit of artistic integrity.

Emmylou Harris' treasured, folk-inspired soprano proved a perfect vehicle for transporting listeners to Appalachia. Her duets with Ricky Skaggs rank with some of her more celebrated harmonic liaisons with Gram Parsons, Herb Pederson, and Rodney Crowell, particularly on "Green Pastures," "Darkest Hour Is Just Before Dawn," and "I'll Go Stepping Too." Rick Skaggs' musical stamp on *Roses in the Snow* is everywhere as a duet or backing vocalist, fiddler, and as a guitar, mandolin, and banjo picker. But Skaggs is not the only illustrious guest. Johnny Cash, Linda Ronstadt and Dolly Parton offer harmony vocals; bluegrass acoustic guitar legend, Tony Rice, the acknowledged master of the dobro, Jerry Douglas, and renowned electric guitarist, Albert Lee, join in; the versatile, country, bluegrass, gospel vocal group, the Whites, add backing vocals; and Willie Nelson appears playing the gut-string guitar. Besides covers of songs penned by bluegrass greats Ralph Stanley, the Louvin Brothers and A.P. Carter, Emmylou Harris sings three traditional numbers including "Wayfaring Stranger," which reached #7 on the *Billboard* single chart. Stretching musical boundaries as Harris was increasingly choosing to do was her lovely bluegrass interpretation Paul Simon's "The Boxer," made more stirringly Appalachian by means of the autoharp played by Bryan Bowers, whose splendid performance throughout the album is impossible to ignore.

As reviewer Razor X, writing in *My Kind of Country*, declared, "The best music is often made when commercial considerations are cast aside, allowing the artist to engage in a labor of love. This is decidedly the case with *Roses in the Snow*." Time and time again, the Americana trailblazers and their disciples have confirmed the accuracy of this conviction. And very few major artists have shattered expectations as dramatically as did Emmylou Harris 15 years later in her 1995 studio release, *Wrecking Ball*.

Produced by Daniel Lanois, best known for his work with U2, Peter Gabriel, Bob Dylan, Neil Young, and Willie Nelson, *Wrecking Ball* featured song treatments and arrangements as far from the country music mainstream as Harris had ever performed. On *Wrecking Ball* are tracks written by Steve Earle ("Goodbye"), Neil Young ("Wrecking Ball"), Bob Dylan ("Every Grain of Sand"), Lucinda Williams ("Sweet Old World"), Gillian Welch ("Orphan Girl"), and, most improbably, Jimi Hendrix ("May This Be Love). On several cuts, Earle and Williams played acoustic guitar and Young added his harmonica and harmony vocals. The record's most compelling ingredient is, of course, Emmylou Harris' singing. Harris' soft, intimate, bare, and inventive vocal renderings evocatively complement the pulsating, percussion-driven production and the richly textured sonic atmosphere orchestrated by Daniel Lanois.

Responses from music critics were much like the following from Trigger, writing in *Saving Country Music*:

> The influence of *Wrecking Ball* is evoked on *Saving Country Music*, and many other country and Americana websites regularly. Its impact on alt-country and Americana may only be undone by Uncle Tupelo's *No Depression*, or Steve Earle's late 80's *Guitar Town*, and may not be outdone by any when it comes to the alt-country subset sometimes described as "progressive" country, or specifically when it comes to influencing the women in alt-country and Americana. And in the nearly 20 years since it was originally released, *Wrecking Ball's* influence hasn't waned a bit, as one female artist after another tries to match or best its watermark. . . *Wrecking Ball* was the result of Emmylou Harris following her heart, searching for a voice she never knew she had, and a vein of country music nobody knew existed before. And even nearly 20 years after its release, its influence, its beauty, and its place as one as one of the most important markers on the country music timeline, remains untarnished.

Given the experimental nature of the album, instead of awarding Emmylou Harris' *Wrecking Ball* with a 1996 Grammy for Best Country Album, the Recording Academy honored it with a 1996 Grammy for Best Contemporary Folk Album. Harris' musically eclectic spirit and genre-blurring sensibilities had firmly taken root and obliged many to refer to her as an Americana rather than a country artist.

The Jayhawks

Alt-country and roots-rock pathfinders, the Minneapolis-nesting Jayhawks, noted for their sweet and sumptuous harmonies, have enjoyed a preeminent perch in the Americana songbook. Led by founders Mark Olson (guitar, harmonica, and vocals) and Gary Louris (guitar and vocals), the Jayhawks produced three albums—*Hollywood Town Hall* (1992), *Tomorrow the Green Grass* (1995), and *Mockingbird Time* (2011)—that especially showcase their distinctive, Gram Parsons/Flying Burrito Brothers-inspired yearnings.

Hollywood Town Hall was the band's first major label release and quickly expanded their popularity beyond the Twin Cities. Instantly distinguished by means of chief songwriters Louris and Olson's heartfelt, transcendent, Everly-Louvin Brothers harmonies, the Jayhawks began to attract a larger and more devoted audience. *Town Hall* incorporates primarily country-tinged melodies, but the Americana artistic urge to blend genres is evident in the occasional power-pop, classic-rock, and folk textures.

The standouts include "Waiting for the Sun," "Two Angels," "Take Me with You When You Go," "Sister Cry," "Clouds," and "Settled Down like Rain," where Cosmic American, Rolling Stones, and Neil Young influences abound, creating a uniquely enchanting synthesis. The musicianship, especially Gary Louris's country guitar picking, is impressive, but with this group it's all about the gorgeous vocals and the crystalline harmonies as *Rolling Stone* magazine's Chris Mundy writes, "When Louris's and Olson's voices rise together, the resulting magic seems like nothing you've heard before." Another *Rolling Stone* reviewer, David Menconi, adds: "When you get right down to it, country music wants to be sad. And there's no more forlorn sound in modern twang-rock than the vocal harmonies of Jayhawks main men Gary Louris and Mark Olson, which could only sound more grief-stricken if Emmylou Harris herself were to sing along."

Tomorrow the Green Grass, the Jayhawks' much-anticipated follow-up to *Hollywood Town Hall*, did not disappoint; in fact, most critics believed it to have surpassed the previous. Reviewer Len Comaratta noted that "the songwriting team of Mark Olson and Gary Louris . . . began fully developing characteristics within their songwriting. Their verses became just as catchy as their choruses, while their slow intros into uptempo songs felt as if two separate songs were juxtaposed." "Blue" and "Two Hearts" display the signature harmonies from Olson and Louris as well as any tracks in the band's impressive songbook. Louris's versatile and masterful guitar licks at times bear resemblance to Dave Davies's power riffs ("Real Light," "Ten Little Kids,") or, at other moments, Clarence White's twang ("See Him on the Street," "Miss William's Guitar"). New keyboardist, Karen Grotberg, proved a worthy addition, adding a fuller sound and more texture to the production. A violin and viola also enhanced the album's depth.

With all apologies to Thomas Wolfe, "you can go home again." Just ask Mark Olson and Karen Grotberg, who, after leaving the band following the release of *Tomorrow* in 1995, returned in 2011 to record the Jayhawks' eighth studio album, *Mockingbird Time*. Gary Louris and Mark Olson wrote all twelve tracks, sounding closer to the Beatles than the Burritos. "Tiny Arrow," "Pouring Rain at Dawn," "Closer to Your Side," and "She Walks in So Many Ways" must be ranked among the Jayhawks' greatest songs. AllMusic reviewer Mark Demming says that "*Mockingbird Time* cuts to the core of what they do best: evocative songs, striking vocals, and a handful of musicians who perform with precision and plenty of heart . . . and serves as a potent reminder that they're one of the finest bands of their time."

Combining introspective lyrics with a unique fusion of alt-country, folk-rock is not going to spike record sales. The market for this kind of music, as pointed out before, is not nearly as comparable in size to the number of fans who follow, as ironic examples, three internationally famous Minneapolis artists—Soul Asylum, the Replacements, and Prince. More connected to their music rather than a *Billboard* chart, the Jayhawks wear their Americana trailblazer influences (Dylan, Parsons, the Byrds, Buffalo Springfield, and the Grateful Dead) on their sleeves yet have integrated their musical inheritance to fashion a sound all their own. In turn, the Jayhawks, despite falling into the under-the-radar category (like Beachwood Sparks), have inspired (cites inflooenz.com) a list of notables, including Will Kimbrough, Neko Case, the National, the Gourds, Tim Easton, Tift Merritt, Kasey Chambers, and Ryan Adams.

Uncle Tupelo

The alt-country movement starts with Uncle Tupelo. So influential was this band that in 1995 the creators of what would become one of the most popular genre magazines chose the title of Uncle Tupelo's debut album, *No Depression*, as its name. Fronted by the most dynamic of duos, singer-songwriters Jay Farrar and Jeff Tweedy, who soon after the band's collapse would form their own highly-acclaimed bands (Son Volt and Wilco), Uncle Tupelo blazed the trail for future musical pioneers.

On their first release, *No Depression* (1990), Uncle Tupelo unleashed a blend of Ramones punk and Gram Parsons country to invent what many see as the first alt-country album. Amanda Petrusich described the record as "a tangling of sensibilities [that] yielded something remarkable: a raw, lonesome, clatter, the singular sound of Midwestern kids getting loud and desperate." The blue-collar themes Petrusich alludes to include alcoholism ("Whiskey Bottle," "Before I Break"); boredom and drudgery ("Graveyard Shift," "Life Worth Livin'," "Factory Belt," "Train"); and the broken heart ("Left in the Dark"). Two upbeat cuts tell of the peace a dying narrator feels in knowing that heaven shortly will be his home ("No Depression") and how the simple life really is not so bad ("Screen Door"). Writing in popmatters.com, Jerrick Adams addresses *No Depression's* resiliency through its punk persona:

> Listening to it now, knowing full well its place in the canon and its impact, *No Depression* remains startling, its aural hallmark being a ferocity that inspires glib punk rock comparisons. These aren't altogether off the mark, of course, but they do gloss over key differences. Where punk rushes forward, thrashes, and bellows, this music by contrast stops and starts, pummels, and howls. Both are intense, but where the sound of the former signifies rage, the sound of *No Depression* signifies something far more tortured and far more painful. . . [Unlike most punk songs] these cuts are nuanced, empathetic, and emotionally resonant.

Expanding their lineup from three to five by adding bassist John Stirratt and multi-instrumentalist Ken Croomer, Uncle Tupelo released their final studio album, *Anodyne* (1993). A harbinger of what was soon to come saw Jay Farrar and Jeff Tweedy no longer sharing songwriting credits. Tension between the two had been mounting as evidenced by a number of verbal and physical altercations. Despite their contentious relationship, the two rivals somehow managed to set aside their differences to produce an extraordinary recording. More country than punk, *Anodyne* mirrors the music of Hank Williams and Merle Haggard much more than it does the Clash or Sex Pistols. Indeed, *Anodyne* is very much classic country. Jay Farrar, interviewed by Richard Cromelin, explained that the band "had explored the loud dynamic for quite some time, so you just try to move on. I guess initially you have a slight aversion to whatever your parents are listening to, just from a rebellion standpoint. But it's always been there peripherally, and eventually you kind of come back to it [traditional country]."

Fiddles, dobros, banjos, steel and acoustic guitars replace the power-chord, garage-rock driven electric guitar riffs from previous Uncle Tupelo recordings as in "Slate," "Acuff-Rose," "Give Back the Key to My Heart," "New Madrid," and "High Water." Only "Chickamauga," "The Long Cut" and "We've Been Had" could have fit comfortably on *No Depression*. (A number of these tracks were later recorded by Farrar's Son Volt and Tweedy's Wilco.) Just as *No Depression* reveals the boundary-pushing, born-to-lead artistic streaks in the two frontmen, so does the more stylistically diverse on *Anodyne*. As reviewer Jason Ankey said: "Recorded live in the studio, the album reinterprets not only country rock but also traditional country, rock, and folk."

The number of artists who influenced Uncle Tupelo is too lengthy to list in its entirety. Among the nine trailblazers, Parsons, the Burritos, the Byrds, and Dylan certainly reverberate lyrically and sonically, but so do Hank Williams, Woody Guthrie, Neil Young, Johnny Cash, and Chuck Berry. Those who have journeyed down Uncle Tupelo's musical path include Drive-by Truckers, Old 97's, and the Bottle Rockets. John M. Tryneski, author of an article titled "Holy Hell! *Anodyne* Turns 20," asks that his readers remember that "for many people Uncle Tupelo's legacy will always be as the group that gave birth to Wilco and Son Volt. It's easy to forget [more importantly] that at the time of their final album they were often looked to as standard-bearers for alternative rock in and of themselves."

Lucinda Williams

A singer-songwriter of extraordinary power, the Lake Charles, Louisiana native ranks at or near the top among Americana's most compelling and treasured musical architects. A 2011 AMA Lifetime Achievement Award and 2015 AMA Album of the Year Award and three Grammys—1993 Best Country Song, 1999 Best Contemporary Folk Album, and 1999 Best Female Rock Vocal Performance—along with over two dozen AMA and Grammy nominations, only begin to underscore her vital role in the Americana music movement.

Like fellow disciples, Mary Chapin Carpenter, Iris DeMent, and Emmylou Harris, Lucinda Williams' voice is immediately recognizable; however, Lucinda has explored more musical genres than these talented contemporaries, including country, rockabilly, country folk, alt-folk, alt-country, blues, country blues, gospel, rock, country rock, folk rock, roots rock, and Americana. Three albums, *Lucinda Williams* (1988), *Sweet Old World* (1992), and, her penultimate release, *Car Wheels on a Gravel Road* (1998), helped to lay the foundation for the Americana movement.

Considered her breakthrough release, *Lucinda Williams* initially flustered some reviewers who struggled with attempts at finding a genre in which to place it. However, most critics, as *Rolling Stone* magazine's Steve Pond reveals here, found Williams to be a captivating artist:

Williams was always on the periphery of L.A.'s vaunted "new country" scene, simply because she's too elusive a talent for narrowcasting: she sings with a down-home twang in her voice, but she also knows her way around Delta-blues songs like Howlin' Wolf's "I Asked for Water (He Gave Me Gasoline)" [the only track among the twelve not composed by Williams] and is capable of writing buoyant pop standouts like "I Just Wanted to See You So Bad" and "Passionate Kisses." She does justice to that full range on *Lucinda Williams*, but there's nothing showy in the way she goes about it. Instead, the album is a low-key, beguiling affair: plain-spoken lyrics, straightforward melodies, simple arrangements . . . you're listening to a singer who is simply telling you the truth about herself. And that's welcome in any genre.

"Passionate Kisses" would become a monster country hit for Mary Chapin Carpenter, and Tom Petty would record "Change the Locks" on his *She's the One* album. Other artists of note have covered cuts from this record: Rodney Crowell/Emmylou Harris ("I Just Wanted to See You So Bad"), Patty Loveless ("The Night's Too Long"), Linda Thomson ("Abandoned"), Johnny Rodriguez ("Big Red Sun Blues"), Ben Folds ("Side of the Road"), and Tim & Mollie O' Brien ("Price to Pay"). As excellent as are these covers, they don't come close to channeling Lucinda Williams' distinctive blend of country and blues sung with the rawest of emotions and in the most sensual of voices.

A meticulous, slow-paced songwriter and a perfectionist in the studio, Lucinda Williams' next album,

Sweet Old World, would not be released until four years later in 1992. The wait, as it turned out, was well worth it as explained by the *Independent's* Andy Gill who called *Sweet Old World* "a revelatory affair, bringing a fresh, raw focus to brilliant songs steeped in lust, death and loss with a blend of sly rockabilly and blues-tinged country-rock." The lust, death, and loss Gill references include "Lines Around Your Eyes," "Hot Blood," "Sweet Old World," "Pineola," "Little Angel, Little Brother," "Something About What Happens When We Talk," "Memphis Pearl," and "Six Blocks Away." Although almost all the tracks disclose painful experiences, "Prove My Love," and "Sidewalks of the City" offer hopeful perspectives on life. Unlike *Lucinda Williams*, very few tracks from *Sweet Old World* (the most ironic of album titles) have been covered by other artists, with the exception of "Sweet Old World," which was recorded by Emmylou Harris. Lucinda Williams' unique singer-songwriter sensibilities were gaining more traction at this time in her career, making it more challenging for those wishing to record her songs. Her inimitable phrasing and raw renderings likely would cause other singers to hesitate from covering a song from this album. In other words, how does one make a Williams song his or her own?

Magnum opus is a term that should rarely be employed when examining an artist's body of work. But, in the case of *Car Wheels on a Gravel Road*, caution can be thrown to the wind. Winner of the 1999 Grammy Award for Best Contemporary Folk Album and the 1998 Pazz & Jop (*Village Voice* magazine) best album prize, *Car Wheels* has deservedly gathered more praise than any Lucinda Williams album before or since. Noted *Rolling Stone* magazine critic, Robert Christgau shared these observations: "Six years in the making, Williams is such a perfectionist that she recorded it from scratch twice . . . always with the perverse goal of making it sound less produced . . . Not only is *Car Wheels on a Gravel Road* more perfect than the two albums that preceded it, which English grammar declares an impossibility, but it achieves its perfection by being more imperfect." From savingcountrymusic.com these accolades:

> The timeline of country music is not delineated by months, years, or decades. It's pinned and articulated by albums and songs that went on to revolutionize the music in some way that was historically and culturally significant, whether the commercial registers were in consensus or not. We're talking about albums such as Willie Nelson's *Red Headed Stranger* and Sturgill Simpson's *Metamodern Sounds in Country Music*. Whatever country music was before, it was something significantly different afterwards. And often over time, reflection bolsters opinions about the significance of these works instead of eroding them, until the making of the albums and the legacy they leave take on an almost mythical status. . . *Car Wheels on a Gravel Road* by Lucinda Williams is one of these such works.

The reviewer adds, "Though its impact would be better to categorize within the Americana sphere instead of country music proper, it was its release and reception that arguably created Americana as a robust and viable creative outlet to counteract country music's more commercial focus."

Lucinda Williams' gritty, achy vocals perfectly match the narrator's carnal memories of a lover in the opening song "Right in Time," seductively establishing the emotional intensity at the heart of *Car Wheels*. In the title track, "Car Wheels on a Gravel Road," the rhythm superbly simulates not only a ride in a car but (ingeniously) the varied emotions and events in childhood. Among many of

Williams' songwriting gifts none may be as important as her adherence to Alexander Pope's poetic principle that "the sound must seem an echo to the sense." Robert Christgau accurately describes Lucinda Williams' voice on *Car Wheels*: "She skillfully deploys the usual roughness tricks, from sandpaper shading to full-scale cracks, but her main techniques are the drawl, emphasized to camouflage or escape her own sophistication, and the sigh, a breathy song-speech that lets her moan or croon or muse or coo or yearn or just feel pretty as the lyric permits and the mood of the moment demands."

Among those artists invited to help out on the recording were Emmylou Harris, who added harmony vocals to "Greenville"; co-producer Steve Earle (acoustic guitar, harmonica, vocals); Buddy Miller (acoustic and electric guitars, vocals); and Jim Lauderdale (vocals). The handpicked musicians possessed the skill set required to contribute to an album that encased such a range of genres. The amalgamation of musical styles, an Americana music benchmark, is on full display: "Lake Charles" (Cajun), "Metal Firecracker" (folk rock), "Jackson" (folk), "Joy" (electric blues), "Concrete and Barbed Wire" (Country), "Can't Let Go" (Delta blues), "I Lost It" (country rock), "2 Kool 2 Be 4-Gotten" (country blues), "Still I Long for Your Kiss" (roots rock), and "Drunken Angel" (rock).

The final commentary on *Car Wheels* and, in general, Lucinda Williams comes from Will Layman, writing for *Spectrum Culture* in 2018, who rhetorically asks, "How does *Car Wheels on a Gravel Road* stand up after 20 years? It hasn't aged a single day for the same reasons that Flannery O'Connor stories don't seem old or that a Rembrandt portrait doesn't seem outdated. The core of Lucinda Williams' art is honesty and detail, with a heaping dose of American musical history. It's the stuff that sticks with you because it's true."

Epilogue

An unavoidable and problematic consequence of generating a list of nine Americana trailblazers is leaving out those artists who deserve the same recognition. As examples, Johnny Cash, Simon & Garfunkel, Neil Young, the Lovin' Spoonful, Creedence Clearwater Revival, Michael Nesmith, Chris Hillman, the Nitty Gritty Dirt Band, among others, are, no doubt, Americana pioneers. Like the nine pathfinders featured in the book, their boundary-pushing, genre-blending, roots-based music unquestionably shaped Americana. The same quandary exists with the nine disciples. Townes Van Zandt, Gillian Welch, Jim Lauderdale, Son Volt, Wico, Tom Petty, John Mellencamp, and Sheryl Crow certainly have followed the trailblazers' footsteps. But the requirement of selecting a handful of names to meet the book's size and scope along with the inherently subjective nature of the process unfortunately created omissions.

Upon reflection, though, such a consequence is not necessarily negative.

Another wonderful feature of Americana music actually is that the probability of finding consensus on identifying the nine (or whatever number chosen) most influential American trailblazers is unlikely. For that matter, whether we should stick an "Americana" tag on a particular artist is often the result of an educated guess at best. All this speaks strongly to the sweeping variety of artists, musical textures, and styles that Americana embraces as compared to other genres. Yet we must not be in a hurry to categorize musical artists, even into the Americana slot. We have seen what happens when Music Row turns its back on musicians who do not match the required mainstream country sound. To employ an "Americana checklist" to determine an artist's "Americana qualifications" would be contrary to everything that this genre represents and must never happen. The "members only" club mentality must be avoided.

Finally, as pointed out early in the book, the word "Americana," officially residing in the *Merriam Webster Dictionary* and enjoying Grammy-category status, goes by an assortment of names (Cosmic American, roots fusion, alt-country, et al). The musical terms utilized throughout *Born to Lead: Americana Music Trailblazers* are, to be clear, of much less importance to the book's greater intent: to familiarize the reader with those artists whose music clearly influenced the Americana music movement specifically and contemporary music in general. The music discussed is what matters most.

As jazz legend Duke Ellington famously commented, "There are two kinds of music—good music and the other kind."

Glossary of Genres

(A list of genres selectively reprinted from KOOP Radio 91.7 FM in Austin, Texas)

Acoustic. Created without the use of electricity.

Alternative. Coined in the early 1980s, the term "alternative rock" or "alternative music" was used to describe music that didn't fit into mainstream genres of the time. Alternative styles include indie, post-punk, hardcore punk, gothic rock, college rock, and new wave bands.

Bluegrass. A form of American roots music with its own roots in the English, Irish and Scottish traditional music of immigrants from the British Isles (particularly the Scots-Irish immigrants of Appalachia), as well as the music of rural African-Americans, jazz, and blues. Like jazz, bluegrass is played with each melody instrument switching off, playing the melody in turn while the others revert to backing; this is in contrast to old-time music, in which all instruments play the melody together or one instrument carries the lead throughout while the others provide accompaniment.

Blues. A vocal and instrumental form of music based on a pentatonic scale and a characteristic twelve-bar chord progression. Blues evolved from African-American spirituals, shouts, work songs, and chants that found its earliest stylistic roots in West Africa and Western popular music, finding expression in ragtime, jazz, big band, R&B, rock and roll, country music, conventional pop songs and even modern classical music.

Cajun. Louisiana music that tends to sound more like early country, with the use of steel guitar and acoustic guitar along with the older, traditional instruments—fiddle, triangle, and accordion. Cajun music is typically a waltz or two step.

Celtic. Celtic music is a broad grouping of musical genres that evolved out of the folk musical traditions of the Celtic peoples of Western Europe. Most typically, the term Celtic music is applied to the music of Ireland and Scotland. The music of Wales, Cornwall, Isle of Man, Brittany, Northumbria and Galicia are also frequently considered a part of Celtic music. Finally, the music of ethnically Celtic peoples abroad are also considered, especially in Canada and the United States.

Classical. Classical music is generally a classification covering music composed and performed by professionally trained artists. Classical music is a written tradition. It is composed and written using music notation, and as a rule is performed faithfully to the score. In common usage "classical music" often refers to orchestral music in general, regardless of when it was composed or for what purposes (film scores and orchestral arrangements on pop music recordings, for example).

Country. Once known as Country & Western music, this music form is developed mostly in the southern United States with roots in traditional folk music, spirituals, and blues.

Dixieland (Jazz). Dixieland developed in New Orleans at the start of the 20th Century and was spread to Chicago and New York City by New Orleans bands in the 1910s, and was, for a period, quite popular among the general public. It is often considered the first true type of jazz and was the the first music referred to by the term "jazz" (before 1917 often spelled "jass").

Experimental. A general term surrounding electronic music without predefined genres.

Folk. Music by and of the common people. Folk music is a down-to-earth style focusing on universal truths, often with traditional acoustic instrumentation and a simple melody. Folk music arose in societies not yet affected by mass communication and the commercialization of culture. It was originally shared and performed by an entire community—not by a special class of expert performers—and was transmitted by word of mouth.

Funk. Funk is a distinct style of music originated by African-Americans, e.g. James Brown and his band members (especially Maceo and Melvin Parker), and groups like the Meters. Funk can be recognized by its syncopated three against four rhythms; thick bass line (often based on an "on the one" beat); razor-sharp rhythm guitars; chanted or hollered vocals (as that of a Marva Whitney of the Bar-Kays); strong rhythm-oriented horn sections; prominent percussion; an upbeat attitude; African tones; danceable; and strong jazz influences (e.g., as in the music of Miles Davis, Herbie Hancock, George Duke, Eddie Harris, and others).

Fusion. At the time of its origin, fusion was a blend of jazz with the aggressive qualities of rock. Today it can represent a blending of any two or more styles.

Garage (Rock). A simple, raw form of rock and roll that emerged in the mid-1960s, largely in the United States. The term "garage rock" comes from the perception that many of the performers were young and amateurish, and often rehearsed in a family garage. Largely inspired by British invasion bands like the Beatles, the Kinks, the Who, and the Rolling Stones, these groups mostly played a homespun variation on British Invasion rock—although other influences were also apparent, especially the surf music style that immediately preceded the garage era. Garage rock was often musically crude, but nevertheless conveyed great passion and energy. Most of the bands used simple chord progressions, pounding drums, and short, repetitive lyrics.

Gospel. Gospel music may refer either to the religious music that first came out of African-American churches in the 1930s or, more loosely, to both black gospel music and to the religious music composed and sung by white Southern Christian artists. While the separation between the two styles was never absolute—both drew from the Methodist Hymnal and artists in one tradition sometimes sang songs belonging to the other—the sharp division between black and white America, particularly black and white churches, kept the two apart. While these divisions have lessened slightly in the last fifty years, the two traditions are still distinct. It tends to be characterized by dominant vocals (often with a strong use of harmony) referencing lyrics of a religious nature.

Honky Tonk. The first genre of music to be commonly known as honky tonk music was a style of piano playing related to ragtime, but emphasizing rhythm more than melody or harmony, since the style evolved in response to an environment where the pianos were often poorly cared for, tending to be out of tune and having some nonfunctional keys.

Indie. A genre of alternative rock that primarily exists in the indie underground music scene. The term is sometimes used interchangeably with indie music as a whole, though more specifically implies that the music meets the criteria of being rock, as opposed to indie pop or other possible matchups. These criteria vary from an emphasis on rock instrumentation (electric guitars, bass guitar, live drums, and vocals) to more abstract (and debatable) rock-and-roll constructions of authenticity.

Jazz. Jazz music has been called the first original art form to develop within the United States. It grew out of a cross-fertilization of folk, blues, ragtime, and European band music. Although there have been many renowned jazz vocalists, and many of the most well-known jazz tunes have lyrics, it is primarily an instrumental form of music. The instrument most closely associated with jazz is the saxophone, followed by the trumpet. The trombone, piano, double bass, guitar, and drums are also primary jazz instruments. It is characterized by blue notes, syncopation, swing, call and response, and polyrhythm, yet the single most distinguishing characteristic of jazz is improvisation. Jazz also tends to utilize complex chord structures and an advanced sense of harmony and requires a high degree of technical skill and musical knowledge from the performers.

Memphis (Blues). Memphis blues is a type of blues that was pioneered in the early part of the 20th Century by musicians like Sleepy John Estes and Willie Nix, who were associated with vaudeville and medicine shows. It was in the Memphis blues that groups of musicians first assigned one guitarist to play rhythm and one to play lead and solos. This has become standard in rock and roll and much of popular music. In addition, the jug band arose out of the Memphis blues, mixing the sound with jazz and using homemade, simple instruments.

Motown. A style of soul music developed in Detroit with distinctive characteristics, including the use of tambourine along with drums, bass instrumentation, a distinctive melodious and chord structure, and call and response singing styles originating in gospel music.

Progressive. Styles that have characteristics from being created by the latest of technology and technique in audio production.

Pop. Pop music is a sub-genre of popular music. Pop music may be distinguished from classical or art music and from folk music, but since the term spans many rock, hip hop, R&B, country, dance, and operatic pop acts, it is reasonable to say that "pop music" is a loosely defined category.

Psychedelic/Trippy. Genres relating to hallucinations, distortions of perception, or altered states of awareness.

Punk. Punk rock is an anti-establishment music movement that began about 1976 (although precursors can be found several years earlier), exemplified by the Ramones, the Sex Pistols, the Clash, and the Damned. The term is also used to describe subsequent music scenes that share key characteristics with those first-generation "punks."

R&B. Rhythm and blues (or R&B) was coined as a musical marketing term in the late 1940s by Jerry Wexler at *Billboard* magazine used to designate upbeat popular music performed by African-American artists who combined jazz and blues. It was initially used to identify the style of music that later developed into rock and roll. By the 1970s, rhythm and blues was being used as a blanket term to describe soul and funk as well. Today, the acronym "R&B" is almost always used instead of "rhythm and blues" and defines the modern version of the soul-and-funk influenced African-American pop music that originated with the demise of disco in 1980.

Ragtime. An American musical genre which enjoyed its peak popularity around the years 1900-1918. Ragtime is a dance form written in 2/4 or 4/4 time and utilizing a walking bass, that is, the bass note played legato on the 1-3 beats with a staccato chord played on the 2-4 beats. Much ragtime is written in sonata form with four distinct themes and a modified first theme appearing in the work. Ragtime music is syncopated with the melodic notes landing largely on the off-beats.

Rock (Rock & Roll). Also called rock 'n' roll, this is a form of popular music, usually featuring vocals (often with vocal harmony), a strong backbeat, electric guitars, and a catchy melody backed by three or four chords.

Rockabilly. Rockabilly is the earliest form of rock and roll as a distinct style of music. It is a fusion of blues, hillbilly boogie, bluegrass, and country music, originating in the American South.

Roots. A term often applied to music closely related to the birth of a genre.

Soul. Soul music is a combination of rhythm and blues and gospel. Rhythm and blues (a term coined by music writer and record producer Jerry Wexler) is itself a combination of blues and jazz and arose in the 1940s as small groups, often playing saxophones, built upon the blues tradition. Soul music is differentiated by its use of gospel-music devices, its greater emphasis on vocalists and merging of religious and secular themes.

Swamp Rock. Another one of Southwest Louisiana's main musical genres, swamp rock is more a combination of many influences and the bridge between Zydeco, New Orleans second line, and rock and roll. The song structure is pure rock and roll, the rhythms are distinctly New Orleans based, the chord changes, vocals, and inflections are R&B-influenced, and the lyrics are sometimes French.

Swing. Swing music, also known as swing jazz, is a form of jazz music that developed during the 1920s and solidified as a distinctive style during the 1930s in the United States. Swing is distinguished primarily by a strong rhythm section, usually including double bass and drums, medium-to-fast tempo, and the distinctive swing time rhythm that is common to many forms of jazz.

Tejano (Tex-Mex). Tejano (Spanish for "Texan") or Tex-Mex music is the various forms of folk and popular music originating among the Mexican-descended Tejanos of Central and South Texas. Usually, Tex-Mex refers to the more traditional styles such as the most popular sub-genre by far, norteno music. Tejano is usually more modern and is heavily influenced by rock, cumbia, and blues.

Zydeco. One of Southwest Louisiana's main musical genres, Zydeco sounds more like gospel or R&B, with artists adopting a James Brown-persona, and instrumentation involving accordion and rub-board washboard along with electronic instruments (guitar and bass), keyboards, drum kit and horns, well suited to the jitterbug.

Essential Recordings

The following albums represent a guide to a better understanding and appreciation of those musical elements associated with Americana music. Included are recommended recordings from the nine trailblazers covered in the book and other artists who best illustrate the Americana style.

      The Band: *Music from Big Pink* (1968), *The Band* (1969), *Stage Fright* (1970).
      The Beau Brummels: *Triangle* (1967), *Bradley's Barn* (1968).
      Beachwood Sparks: *Beachwood Sparks* (2000), *Once We Were Trees* (2001).
      The Beatles: *Rubber Soul* (1965).
      Billy Bragg & Wilco: *Mermaid Avenue* (1998).
      Jackson Browne: *Jackson Browne* (1972), *For Everyman* (1973), *Late For the Sky* (1974), *Running on Empty* (1977).
      Buffalo Springfield: *Buffalo Springfield Again* (1967), *Last Time Around* (1968).
      The Byrds: *Fifth Dimension* (1966), *Younger Than Yesterday* (1967), *The Notorious Byrd Brothers* (1968), *Sweetheart of the Rodeo* (1968), *Dr. Byrds and Mr. Hyde* (1969), *(Untitled)*, 1970.
      Mary Chapin Carpenter: *Come On Come On* (1992), *Stones in the Road* (1994), *The Age of Miracles* (2010).
      Johnny Cash: *American Recordings* (1994).
      Rosanne Cash: *The Wheel* (1993), *Black Cadillac* (2006), *The List* (2009), *The River & the Thread* (2014).

Ray Charles: *Modern Sounds in Country and Western Music* (1962).

Gene Clark: *Gene Clark with the Gosdin Brothers* (1967), *White Light* (1971), *No Other* (1974).

Elvis Costello: *Almost Blue* (1981).

Creedence Clearwater Revival: *Bayou Country* (1969), *Green River* (1969), *Willy and the Poor Boys* (1969), *Cosmo's Factory* (1970).

David Crosby: *If I Could Only Remember My Name* (1971).

Crosby, Stills & Nash: *Crosby, Stills & Nash* (1969).

Crosby, Stills, Nash & Young: *Déjà vu* (1970).

Rodney Crowell: *The Houston Kid* (1970), *Fate's Right Hand* (2003), *The Outsider* (2005).

Sheryl Crow: *Sheryl Crow* (1996), *Be Myself* (2017).

Iris DeMent: *Infamous Angel* (1992), *My Life* (1994), *Sing the Delta* (2012).

The Desert Rose Band: *The Desert Rose Band* (1987), *Running* (1988).

Dillard & Clark: *The Fantastic Expedition of Dillard & Clark* (1968), *Through the Morning, Through the Night* (1969).

Bob Dylan: *Bringing It All Back Home* (1965), *Highway 61 Revisited* (1965), *Blonde on Blonde* (1966), *John Wesley Harding* (1967), *Nashville Skyline* (1969).

Bob Dylan & The Band: *The Basement Tapes* (1975).

Steve Earle: *Guitar Town* (1986), *Copperhead Road* (1988), *Train a Comin'* (1995), *I Feel Alright* (1996), *El Corazon* (1997).

Steve Earle & The Del McCoury Band: *The Mountain* (1998).

Fairport Convention: *Unhalfbricking* (1969), *Liege & Lief* (1969).

The Flying Burrito Brothers: *The Gilded Palace of Sin* (1969), *Burrito Deluxe* (1970).

Jimmy Dale Gilmore: *Spinning Around the Sun* (1993), *Braver New World* (1996).

The Grateful Dead: *Workingman's Dead* (1970), *American Beauty* (1970).

Arlo Guthrie: *Alice's Restaurant* (1967), *Washington County* (1970), *Hobo's Lullaby* (1972), *Last of the Brooklyn Cowboys* (1974).

Woody Guthrie: *The Asch Recordings* (1944 &1945).

Merle Haggard: *Swinging Doors* (1966), *I'm a Lonesome Fugitive* (1967), *Sing Me Back Home* (1968), *The Legend of Bonny & Clyde* (1968), *Mama Tried* (1968), *Pride in What I Am* (1969), *Same Train, A Different Time* (1969), *Hag* (1971), *Someday We'll Look Back* (1971).

Emmylou Harris: *Pieces of the Sky* (1975), *Elite Hotel* (1975), *Luxury Liner* (1976), *Quarter Moon in a Ten Cent Town* (1978), *Roses in the Snow* (1980), *Wrecking Ball* (1995).

Chris Hillman & Herb Pederson: *Bakersfield Bound* (1996).

Hot Rize: *Hot Rize* (1979), *Traditional Ties* (1986), *Untold Stories* (1987).

The International Submarine Band: *Safe at Home* (1968).

The Jayhawks: *Hollywood Town Hall* (1992), *Tomorrow the Green Grass* (1995), *Mockingbird Time* (2011).

Jefferson Airplane: *Surrealistic Pillow* (1967), *Volunteers* (1969).

Waylon Jennings: *Lonesome, On'ry and Mean* (1973), *Honky Tonk Heroes* (1973), *This Time* (1974), *Waylon Live* (1976), *Greatest Hits* (1979).

Valerie June: *Pushin' Against a Stone* (2013), *The Order of Time* (2017).

The Louvin Brothers: *Tragic Songs of Life* (1956), *Satan Is Real* (1959).

Love: *Love* (1966), *Da Capo* (1966), *Forever Changes* (1967),

The Lovin' Spoonful: *Hums of the Lovin' Spoonful* (1966).

Manassas: *Manassas* (1972).

John Mellencamp: *No Better Than This* (2010), *Plain Spoken* (2014).

Moby Grape: *Moby Grape* (1967).

Bill Monroe: *The Music of Bill Monroe* (1994).

Mumford & Sons: *Babel* (2012).

Willie Nelson: *Red Headed Stranger* (1975).

New Riders of the Purple Sage: *New Riders of the Purple Sage* (1971).

The Nitty Gritty Dirt Band: *Uncle Charlie & His Dog Teddy* (1970), *Will the Circle Be Unbroken* (1972).

Buck Owens and His Buckaroos: *Together Again* (1964), *I've Got a Tiger by the Tail* (1965), *Carnegie Hall Concert* (1966).

Gram Parsons: *GP* (1973), *Grievous Angel* (1974), *Sleepless Nights* (1976).

Tom Petty: *Full Moon Fever* (1989), *Wildflowers* (1994).

Poco: *Pickin' Up the Pieces* (1969), *Poco* (1970), *Deliverin'* (1971), *Crazy Eyes* (1973).

John Prine: *John Prine* (1971), *Diamonds in the Rough* (1972), *Sweet Revenge* (1973), *Bruised Orange* (1978), *The Missing Years* (1991), *In Spite of Ourselves* (1999).

The Rolling Stones: *Exile on Main Street* (1972).

The Seldom Scene: *Act III* (1973).

Son Volt: *Trace* (1995), *Honky Tonk* (2013).

Richard and Linda Thompson: *I Want to See the Bright Lights Tonight* (1974), *Shoot Out the Lights* (1982).

Uncle Tupelo: *No Depression* (1990), *Anodyne* (1993).

Townes Van Zandt: *Our Mother the Mountain* (1969), *Townes Van Zandt* (1969), *Delta Momma Blues* (1971), *High, Low and In Between* (1972).

Doc Watson: *Doc Watson* (1964), *Southbound* (1966).

Gillian Welch: *Time (The Revelator)* (2001), *The Harrow & The Harvest* (2011).

Wilco: *Being There* (1996), *Summerteeth* (1999), *Yankee Hotel Foxtrot* (2001), *A Ghost Is Born* (2004), *Star Wars* (2015).

Hank Williams: *40 Greatest Hits* (1978).

Lucinda Williams: *Lucinda Williams* (1988), *Sweet Old World* (1992), *Car Wheels on a Gravel Road* (1998), *World Without Tears* (2003), *Down Where the Spirit Meets the Bone* (2014), *The Ghosts of Highway 20* (2016).

Neil Young: *Everybody Knows This Is Nowhere* (1969), *After the Gold Rush* (1970), *Harvest* (1972), *Comes a Time* (1979).

Bibliography

Adams, Jerrick. "Uncle Tupelo: *No Depression*." Popmatters.com. Web. 5 October 2018.

Alden, Grant. "Steve Earle: *El Corazon*." October 31, 1997. Nodepression.com. Web. 4 October 2018.

"Americana Artists." Last.fm. Web. 16 September 2018.

Ankeny, Jason. "Uncle Tupelo: *Anodyne*." Allmusic.com. Web. 5 October 2018.

The Anvil, "*Common Sense*." Theanvilreview.org. February 27, 2010. Web. 12 September 2018.

"Arlo Guthrie Quotes." Brainyquote.com. Web. 7 September 2018.

Barkhorn, Eleanor. "How Bob Dylan Changed the '60s, and American Culture." Theatlantic.com. September 9, 2010. Web. 17 July 2018.

Bass, Rick. "The Ballad of John Prine." Mensjournsal.com. Web. 14 September 2018.

"Beachwood Sparks: An L.A. Story, Past & Present." Aquariumdrunkard.com. Web. 26 September 2018.

Berg, Karen. "*John Prine*." Rollingstone.com. December 23, 1971. Web. 10 September 2018.

Bradley, William. "*Buffalo Springfield Again*." Huffpost.com. November 27, 2017. Web. 30 August 2018.

Brendan. "Gene Clark *White Light*." Therisingstrom.net. Nov 28, 2007. Web. 25 August 2018.

Cain, Michaele Scott. *The Americana Revolution: From Country and Blues Roots to the Avett Brothers,*

Mumford & Sons, and Beyond. New York: Rowman & Littlefield, 2017.

Comaratta, Len. "Dusting 'Em Off: The Jayhawks—*Tomorrow the Green Grass*." Consequencesofsound.net. September 17, 2011. Web. 5 October 2018.

Cash, Jonny with Patrick Carr. *Cash*. New York: HarperCollins, 2003.

Chilton, Martin. "Americana: How Country and Roots Music Found a 'Brand New Dance.'" Udiscovermusic.com. May 1, 2018. Web. 12 July 2018.

Chilton, Martin. "Bob Dylan's 25 Musical Heroes, Including Guy Clark." May 17, 2016. Web. 24 August 2018.

Chilton, Martin. "How the Flying Burrito Brothers Hit the Jackpot with *The Gilded Palace of Sin*." Udiscovermusic.com. May 9, 2018. Web. 11 August 2018.

Christgau, Robert. "*Car Wheels on a Gravel Road*." Rolllingstone.com. June 18, 1998. Web. 8 October 2018.

Classic Albums—The Grateful Dead: Anthem to Beauty (DVD). Rhino/WEA. 1999.

"Country Pop Reborn under the Desert Sky." Thecalmingseas.com. Web. 27 September 2018.

Cromelin, Richard. "Uncle Tupelo's *Anodyne*." Articles.latime.com. November 10, 1993. Web. 6 October 2018.

Crusadercob. "Jerry Garcia and the Pedal Steel Guitar." Nodepression.com. August 20, 2012. Web. 3 September 2018.

Deming, Mark. "*Burrito Deluxe*." Allmusic.com. Web. 22 August 2018.

Deming, Mark. "The Jayhawks: *Mockingbird Time*." Allmusic.com. Web. 5 October 2018.

Deming, Mark. "*Sweetheart of the Rodeo*." Allmusic.com. Web. 2 August 2018.

Dennis, Eric. "Revisit: Steve Earle: *Train a Comin'*." Spectrumculture.com. August 29, 2011. Web. 3 October 2018.

DeRiso, Nick. "Exploring Deep Cuts from the Band's Underrated *Stage Fright*." Somethingelsereviews.com. Web. 25 September 2018.

Deusner, Stephen M. "Beachwood Sparks: *Desert Skies*." Pitchfork.com. November 27, 2013. Web. 26 September 2018.

Eder, Bruce. "The Shilos." Allmusic.com. Web. 13 August 2018.

Erlewine, Stephen Thomas. "The Band: *Music from Big Pink*." Pitchfork.com. September 1, 2018. Web. 22 September 2018.

Erlewine, Stephen Thomas. "*The Freewheelin' Bob Dylan*." Allmusic.com. Web. 16 July 2018.

Feuer, Daiana. "Emmylou Harris. Truth Is Still There." Larecord.com. September 15, 2016. Web. 9 October 2018.

Flanagan, Bill. "Bob Dylan Exclusive Interview: Reveals His Favorite Songwriters, Thoughts on His Own Cult Figure Status." Huffpost.com. April 15, 2009. Web. 9 September 2018.

Forman, Bill. "Richie Furay on Buffalo Springfield, Poco and the Roots of Americana. August 23, 2017. Web. 20 August 2018.

Frater, Bill. "My First Non-DJ: Americana Promoter Al Moss." Nodepression.com. Web. 25 July 2018.

Fremer, Michael. "Remembering Gene Clark." Analogplanet.com. March 31, 2012. Web. 24 August 2018.

Fricke, David and Robert Christgau, "50 Essential Albums of 1967." Rollingstone.com. September 19, 2017. Web. 1 August 2018.

Fry, Peggy. "Album Review—Mary Chapin Carpenter, *The Age of Miracles*." Twistedkite.net. February 22, 2011. Web. 28 September 2018.

Gallacher, Alex. "UK Americana Awards 2018: Awards and Nominees." Folkradio.co.uk. January 4, 2018. Web. 15 September 2018.

Gates, Guilbert. "Listen to Bob Dylan's Many Influences." Nytimes.com. October 15, 2016. Web. 28 July 2018.

"Genres & Definitions." KOOP Radio 91.7 FM. Koop.org. Web. 17 September 2018.

Giles, Jeff. "Richie Furay Admits Frustration Over Aborted Buffalo Springfield Reunion." Ultimateclassicrock.com. May 13, 2015. Web. 30 August 2018.

Gill, Andy. "Lucinda Williams, *This Sweet Old World.*" Independent.co.uk. October 19, 2017. Web. 7 October 2018.

Gill, Andy. "Back to the Land." *Mojo Magazine*. November 2000. Theband.hiof.no. Web. 16 September 2018.

Gilmore, Mikal. "Why Bob Dylan Is a Literary Genius." Rollingstone.com. December 9, 2016. Web. 18 July 2018.

Gleason, Holly. "Mary Chapin Carpenter: *Come On Come On*." Americansongwriter.com. April 30, 2010. Web. 27 September 2018.

Gleason, Ralph J. "*The Band*." Rollingstone.com. October 18, 1969. Web. 24 September 2018.

Green, Andy. "Stephen Stills Breaks Silence on Short-Lived Buffalo Springfield Reunion." Rollingstone.com. November 5, 2012. Web. 29 August 2018.

Green, Andy. "Stephen Stills Looks Back at Buffalo Springfield: 'I Have No Regrets.'" Rollingstone.com. May 30, 2018. Web. 29 August 2018.

Harris, Craig. The Band: Pioneers of Americana Music. Lanham, Maryland: Rowman & Littlefield, 2014.

Helm, Levon with Stephen Davis. *This Wheel's on Fire: Levon Helm and the Story of the Band*. Chicago: Chicago Review Press, 1993.

Hermes, Will. "How Bob Dylan's *Bringing It All Back Home* 'Stunned the World'." Rollingstone.com. March 22, 2016. Web. 16 July 2018.

Hernandez, Raoul. "Beachwood Sparks: *Once We Were Trees*." Austinchronicle.com. October 26, 2001. Web. 28 September 2018.

Hight, Jewly. "Infamous Angel: A Q&A with Iris DeMent." Americansongwriter.com. October 8, 2012. Web. 1 October 2018.

"The History of the Americana Music Association." Americanamusic.org. Web. 12 July 2018.

Hundley, Jessica with Polly Parsons. *Grievous Angel: An Intimate Portrait of Gram Parsons*. New York: Thunder's Mouth, 2005.

Jackson, Andrew Grant. 1965: *The Most Revolutionary Year in Music*. New York: Thomas Dunne, 2015.

"The Jayhawks Influences." Infllenz.com. Web. 5 October 2018.

Joffe, Justin. "Did Neil Young Really Kill Buffalo Springfield? Observer.com. December 6, 2016. Web. 29 August 2018.

"John Prine Quotes." Azquotres.com. Web. 7 September 2018.

Jurek, Thom. "*No Other*." AllMusic.com. Web. 27 August 2018.

Jurek, Thom. "*White Light*." Allmusic.com. Web. 26 August 2018.

Keefe, Jonathan. Iris DeMent: *Sing the Delta*. Slantmagazine.com. November 4, 2012. Web. 2 October 2018.

Kot, Greg. "The Grateful Dead: The Band That Could Save Music." Bbc.com. July 1. 2015. Web. 8 September 2018.

Krerowicz, Aaron. "Bob Dylan's Influence on the Beatles." Aaronkrerowicz.com February 2, 2013. Web.

Layman, Will. "Holy Hell! *Car Wheels on a Gravel Road Turns 20*." Spectrumculture.com. June 20, 2018. Web. 9 October 2018.

Lesh, Phil. *Searching for the Sound*. New York: Little Brown, 2005.

"Levon Helm Quotes." Brainyquote.com. Web. 6 August 2018.

Lewis, Randy. Byrds Founding Member Gene Clark to Be Saluted Saturday in South Pasadena. Latimes.com. Feb. 24, 2017. Web. 27 August 2018.

Lindsay, Andrew. "Interview: Neal Casal (Ryan Adams & the Cardinals)." Stereokill.net. April 19, 2009. Web. 27 September 2018.

Little, Michael H. "Graded on a Curve: John Prine, *John Prine*." Thevinyldistrict.com. November 22, 2013. Web. 10 September 2018.

Lipson, Harry. "How Do You Define Americana Music?" Nodepression.com. June 11, 2013. Web 16 July 2018.

"Look Out Cleveland." Songmango.com. Web. 24 September 2018.

Menconi, David. "The Jayhawks, *Hollywood Town Hall* (1992)" from "50 Rock Albums Every Country Fan Should Own." Rollingstone.com. November 12, 2014. Web. 5 October 2018.

Martin, Gavin. "Buffalo Springfield: Back in the Summer of '67." Independent.co.uk. June 22, 2001. Web. 30 August 2018.

McKeen, William. *Everybody Had and Ocean: Music and Mayhem in 1960s Los Angeles*. Chicago: Chicago Review Press, 2017.

Meyer, David N. Meyer. *Twenty Thousand Roads: The Ballad of Gram Parsons and His Cosmic American Music.* New York: Villard, 2007.

"Michael Clarke—*Full Circle* Magazine 1991." *The Byrds Lyrics Page/Interviews.* Die-augenweide.de. Web. 27 August 2018.

Miller, Joshua. "Steve Earle Revisits His Rock Opus *Copperhead Road* 30 Years Later." Shepherdexpress.com. March 27, 2018. Web. 3Otober 2018.

Mills, Gordon. "*John Wesley Harding.*" Rollingstone.com. February 24, 1968. Web. 17 July 2018.

Morris, Edward. "Rodney Crowell: Sitting at *Fate's Right Hand.*" Cmt.com. August 25, 2003. Web. 29 September 2018.

Moss, Marissa R. "The Alchemy of John Prine." Nashvillescene.com. April 12, 2018. Web. 14 September 2018.

Mundy, Chris. "The Jayhawks: *Hollywood Town Hall.* Webarchive.org. (*Rolling Stone* magazine). June 29, 2001. Web. 4 October 2018.

Nash, Alanna. "*My Life.*" Ew.com. April 15, 1994. Web. 1 October 2018.

Neekafat. "Mary Chapin Carpenter: *Stones in the Road.*" Sputnikmusic.com. February 2, 2017. Web. 28 September 2018.

Nolan, Jeff. "Artist of the Month—Sheryl Crow." Hardrock.com. May 2, 2017. Web. 26 September 2018.

Nolan, Tom. "*Sweet Revenge.*" Rollingstone.com. January 31, 1974. Web. 13 September 2018.

Okamoto, David. "Iris DeMent: *My Life.*" Webarchive.org. (*Rolling Stone* magazine). August 11, 1994. Web 2 October 2018.

"100 Best Albums of the Eighties." Rollingstone.com. November 16, 1989. Web. 2 October 2018.

Paterson, Beverly. "The Byrds' *Turn! Turn! Turn!* Offered a Message of Hope in Troubled Time." Somethingelsereviews.com. Web. 22 July 2018.17 July 2018.

Petrusich, Amanda. "Uncle Tupelo: *No Depression*: Legacy Edition." Pitchfork.com. January 30, 2014. Web. 5 October 2018.

Power, Tom. "25 Best Canadian Debut Albums Ever." Cbcmusic.ca. June 16, 2017. Web. 17 September, 2018.

Proehl, Bob. "Time for a Repress: ‘ *The Gilded Palace of Sin* #8217;" Popmatters.com. March 29, 2009. Web. 13 August 2018.

Rabin, Nathan. "Where to Start with the Father of 'Cosmic American Music,' Gram Parsons." Avclub.com. June 6, 2012. Web. 23 August 2018.

Razor X. "Album Review: Emmylou Harris—*Roses in the Snow*." Mykindofcountry.wordpress.com. April 15, 2011. Web. 10 October 2018.

Reed, Patrick A. "Americana Chronicle: Arlo Guthrie, 1970-176." Depthoffieldmagazine.com. March 5, 2011. Web. 6 September 2018.

Richards, Keith with James Fox. *Life*. New York: Little, Brown. 2010.

Rogan, Johnny. "Gene Clark's Irish Catholic Roots Uncovered." Irishtimes.com. August 24, 2017. Web. 26 August 2018.

"Roger McGuinn Quotes." Brainyquote. Web. 11 August 2018.

"Roger Waters Quote Re *Music from Big Pink*." Prog Archives. April 27, 2008. Web. 16 September 2018.

Savage, John. *1966: The Year the Decade Exploded*. London: Faber & Faber, 2015.

Scoppa, Bud. "Emmylou Harris—Album by Album." Uncut.co.uk. January 25, 2013. Web. 9 October 2018.

Sexton, Paul. "U.K. Americana Hits America, and Vice Versa, in New Roots Exchange." Billboard.com. October 10, 2017. Web. 15 September 2018.

Simpson, Dave. "The Byrds: How We Made 'Eight Miles High'." Theguardian.com. September 16, 2014. Web. 27 July 2018.

"'Singing Is Praying' for Iris DeMent." Npr.org. October 28, 2012. Web. 1 October 2018.

Snapes, Laura. "There's a Hunger for the Next Frontier: the New Cosmic Americana." Theguardian.com. July 28, 2016. Web. 27 September 2018.

Streissguth, Michael. *Outlaw: Waylon, Willie, Kris, and the Renegades of Nashville*. New York: itbooks, 2013.

"Steve Earle Influences." Inflooenz.com. Web. 5 October 2018.

Strickler, Yancey. "Beachwood Sparks: *Once We Were Trees*." Neumu.net. Web. 28 September 2018.

Swanson, Dave. "50 Years Ago: The Byrds Transform on *The Notorious Byrd Brothers*." Ultimateclassicrock.com. January 15, 2015. Web. 5 August 2018.

Thanki, Juli. "John Prine: The Godfather of Americana Music." Tenssean.com. September 12, 2017. Web. 13 September 2018.

"This Music Made Me: Mary Chapin Carpenter." Musicomh.com. May 30, 2016. Web. 24 September 2018.

Trigger. "The Lingering Influence of Emmylou's *Wrecking Ball*." Savingcountrymusic.com. March 22, 2014. Web. 11 October 2018.

Trigger. "Vintage Album Review—Lucinda Williams' *Car Wheels on a Gravel Road*." Savingcountrymusic.com. June 28, 2018. 8 October 2018.

"Top Psychedelic Albums No. 19: *Fifth Dimension*." Psychedelicsight.com. September 14, 2012. Web. 28, July 2018.

Tryneski, John M. "Holy Hell! *Anodyne* Turns 20." Spectrumculture.com. April 3, 2013. Web. 6 October 2018.

Unterburger, Richie. "Chris Hillman Interview." Web. 10 August 2018.

Wener, Ben. "Buffalo Springfield Stunningly Returns to L.A." ocregister.com. June 6, 2011. Web. 30 August 2018.

"What Is Cosmic American Music? (And a List of Examples)." Nodepression.com. March 21, 2018. Web. 26 September 2018.

Willman, Chris. "Bob Weir Grateful to Get Back in Touch with His Cowboy Side at Americana Fest." Billboard.com. September 23, 2016. Web. 20 August 2018.

Woodward, Jake, et al. *Grateful Dead: The Illustrated Trip*. London: Dorling Kindersley Limited, 2003.

"Word Interview Exclusive: Roger Waters." *The Word*. April 13, 2008. Web. 9 September 2018.

Wosahla, Steve. "My Favorite Album: Jim Lauderdale on Gram Parsons' *Grievous Angel*." Nodepression.com. August 22, 2015. Web. 22 August 2018.

The Author

This is Mark Hodermarsky's eighth book and follows his most recent title, *The Animals: True Rock Royalty*, also from New Haven Publishing. Hodermarsky has authored or edited six other books: *The Cleveland Sports Legacy Since 1945*; *The Cleveland Sports Legacy, 1900-1945*; *The Toe: The Lou Groza Story (with Lou Groza)*; *The Object of the Game (with Chuck Kyle)*; *Baseball's Greatest Writers*; and *Beyond Trochenbrod: The Betty Gold Story (with Betty Gold)*.

He has served as a book critic for the *Cleveland Plain Dealer* and has contributed numerous articles to a variety of publications.

Hodermarsky lives in Olmsted Falls, Ohio, a Cleveland suburb.

Lightning Source UK Ltd.
Milton Keynes UK
UKHW041514181118
332549UK00003B/25/P